FREEDOM—WHEN?

FREEDOM

Random House   New York

WHEN?

by James Farmer

with an introduction by Jacob Cohen

TO

My father,
   One generation from bondage,
      Did he understand?

And my daughters, Tami and Abbey,
      Will they understand?

*If we are not for ourselves,
who will be?*

*If we are only for ourselves,
of what worth are we?*

If not now, when?

PREFACE

For the men and women of CORE and their brothers in the great "movement" the cry *"Freedom Now!"* was no mere slogan. Quite literally did we demand that equality and freedom come to this land, immediately. We would permit no delay. With our very bodies we would obstruct the wheels of injustice; by our eloquence and ineluctable presence we would teach a callous public of the inhumanities its complacency condoned. (How could they resist the truth once they saw it?) To smash the thrall of unconstitutional laws and immoral legal practices we would fill the jails to bursting, if necessary. We would act directly on the institutions and especially upon the evildoer, negotiating, persuading, cajoling, giving him no rest.

If only the might of wanting, and the will to act, and

purity of purpose could change all things, *Now* would be today.

But we are learning that freedom will not be now. CORE has changed over the years. In many ways our sights have shifted and our priorities have altered. Once a middle-class cadre of idealists, militantly opposed to the external symbols of segregation and discrimination, we have become increasingly a mass movement, our attention turned inward to the ghetto—our support, our leaders, our goals, our temper, set by the people of the ghetto. Direct action—picketing, boycotts, demonstrations, sit-ins—no longer seem so central to our effort. But can we drop direct action altogether? Our techniques are more varied and great questions of strategy and tactics loom.

What does "integration" mean today and how satisfactorily does the term define our goals? How shall we enter politics and use politicians well and yet resist being used for ill? Can a CORE rooted in the ghetto avoid the allure of black nationalism? What remains useful in the philosophy of non-violence? What friends do we need and what friends do we have? What role do the various civil rights organizations play in the fight for freedom? How can we contribute to the solutions of problems looming "beyond civil rights" —such as poverty, unemployment, and the various lacks in training and motivations of black Americans—which refuse to wait until discrimination and segregation are finally eliminated? What dangers do we face from communist and other subversions?

We are settling down for a longer haul than we thought necessary, and in the midst of things I have felt the need to understand the present by reclaiming the past and seizing upon the future.

I have incurred many debts of gratitude during the writing of this book and I would like to begin paying them. Douglas Levin of Local 99, ILGWU, provided me with a sanctuary in the form of a quiet office away from the bustle where I could work and reflect. The members of Local 99 have been exceedingly generous to CORE in the past and this particular kindness to me was much appreciated. Meryl Mann, an expert writer, provided expert editorial assistance. My friend Jacob Cohen of Brandeis University, whom I have asked to write the introduction to this book, read the manuscript with a most critical and discerning eye, as did Alan Gartner. Marvin Rich, of the CORE Scholarship, Education, and Defense Fund, who forgets nothing, several times reminded me of a detail I had forgotten or distorted in the remembering. Linda Umans was a most excellent typist. And, of course, my wife, Lula, without whom . . .

CONTENTS

Preface   *ix*

Introduction   *xvii*

A Southern Tale   3

". . . But When Will the
   Demonstrations End?"   23

We Are Soldiers   51

Black Nationalists and White Liberals   83

Integration or Desegregation   109

Africa Revisited   129

Freedom—When?   167

INTRODUCTION

No term describes better the daily labor of James Farmer than "Spokesman." Since 1961, when he left the NAACP to become CORE's National Director, Farmer has been a spokesman for CORE, the "Movement," the Negro People, and even the conscience of mankind, depending upon the occasion. These occasions arise many times a day or night. He is on stage almost continually, often badly in need of sleep and the memory of some recent quiet. There is always another street-corner rally to be cheered on, swarming, ubiquitous reporters demanding quotable comments, a televised news conference under glaring lights before four inquisitors, each hoping to trap him into the damaging confession, the hidden contradiction, the flicker of uncertainty, which make headlines.

Farmer must be a spokesman in manner as well as word: feet must not ache when he walks on picket lines; dignity must not flee when husky policemen, each tugging one of his brown limbs, drag him off to a paddy wagon; and though he is warned continually by the FBI and state and local police of plots against his life, and he must often remember the time he tells of in this book when he was in

such danger that for hours he expected to die, still fear must
not show in the fierce eyes nor halt the flow of astonishingly
resonant and superbly articulated speech which is his hall-
mark. He knows that he must be slightly larger than life,
representing in his person some of the spirit and command
of the Negro movement. Yet one of the engaging qualities
James Farmer reveals in this book is his ability to view the
requirements of his job with a sense of humor and propor-
tion.

For better or worse, the rules of what we might term
"spokesmanship" govern the presentation to the public of
every cause and organized movement. There is not now
an exception to the rule nor is any in sight, so there is no
sense in challenging its sway. As soon expect Farmer to
confess on television to some momentary unworthiness in
CORE as to have expected that Adlai Stevenson would
confess before the UN misgivings over American policy in
Vietnam and the Dominican Republic. The dedicated
spokesman knows that the Truth of the cause he serves permits some salesmanship. Second thoughts and first ones are
for the tent, not for the battlefield, where ambivalence is
deemed fatal, and the most effective leadership takes place
out of public sight, emancipated from the necessity of making a spectacle of itself.

All the more notable, then, is the fact that in this book,
his first, James Farmer permits the reader to eavesdrop on
the debate raging within the civil rights tent today, and
to observe the most worthy ambivalence of one of the
movement's principal leaders.

Make no mistake. This is a public book, filled with stirring affirmations as it must be. But significantly, the CORE
to which Farmer here affirms, or rather reaffirms his commitment, is a CORE very different from that romantic little
organization which in 1961 freedom-rode through the

South and began training new cadres in the techniques of non-violence. Indeed the movement itself, or at least that important part of it which CORE represents, has taken a course of late which few would have predicted or approved of a few years ago. In defending the honor of these developments, Farmer enters into a strenuous and most revealing debate with CORE's own traditions and with critics in and out of the movement. The result, as the reader will find, is,

—A tight-fisted and almost pragmatic statement of the philosophy of non-violence (also a justification for armed self-defense in certain circumstances), which is quite different from the loving exhortations to which Martin Luther King and an older CORE habituated us.
—A celebration of Negro group pride and group aspiration, which amounts to a virtual transvaluation of the ideal of integration.
—A sharper clash than we have yet seen with rival philosophies and philosophers in the movement, including debates with Roy Wilkins, whom Farmer chides for being mired in the past; Bayard Rustin, who, he thinks, is mired in the future; the late Malcolm X, who, we learn, was wrong for the right reasons.
—And reflections on the meaning of Freedom which sum up the most valuable experiences and lessons gleaned from this last tumultuous decade.

From the evidence of this book, Farmer has not discarded his old faith easily. He confesses to some scars of passage and even to a hint of nostalgia for simpler days. And this is further evidence that he is not only the first spokesman for a new Negro mood in America, but also a man and leader of depth.

Like Lyndon Baines Johnson, James Leonard Farmer, Jr.,

is a Texan. Born in Marshall, Texas, January 12, 1920, he was the first son and second of three children of the former Pearl Houston and Dr. J. Leonard Farmer, an old Testament scholar, minister of the Gospel, and the first Negro Ph.D. in the state.

Like many Negro fathers, J. Leonard Farmer had a remarkable family history to bequeath to his children. He was born in Kingstree, South Carolina, to former slaves, and at an early age moved with the family by mule and buggy to Pearson, Georgia. There his father worked, tapping trees for turpentine in the pine forests, until he went blind. The family story has it that Grandfather's blindness resulted from peering steadily up the trunks of pine trees into the sun, searching for a suitable spot to sink his tap. Farmer seems taken with the image.

There was no high school in the state open to Negroes at the time, so when Farmer, Sr., finished his elementary schooling in a rural shack, he walked all the way to the Bethune-Cookman Institute in Daytona Beach, Florida, where he had been awarded a scholarship. Some time later, after achieving an outstanding record at the Institute, he walked, knapsack on back, to Boston, where he had been accepted at Boston University. Again he achieved a brilliant record, despite the fact that while he attended school he worked part-time as a valet and carriage boy for a wealthy woman in order to support himself and his family. He was graduated *magna cum laude* and in two years completed work for a Ph.D. at Boston University's School of Theology, with a thesis which ventured a redating and re-interpretation of some passages from Deutero-Isaiah.

James Farmer grew up in his father's library, in the protected atmosphere of the Negro colleges where his father taught. First at Wiley College in Marshall, where he was born; then almost immediately at Rust College in Holly

Springs, Mississippi; five years later at Samuel Houston, a methodist school in Austin, Texas; and five years after that at the Gammon Theological Seminary in Atlanta for three years; and in 1933 back to Wiley, from which he was to graduate in 1938. While he grew up in the South, Farmer was cut off from the conflict and pain of the general Negro community. He lived in a scholar's house, and like the children of most scholars he suffered mostly from disquisitions on fine points of scholarly dispute. He cannot recall a time when his father went to the movies. He preferred, Farmer says, to sit under a tree and read a book written in Greek or Latin or Aramaic or German or French. The only white people Farmer came into contact with were other academics or salesmen who came to the campus wishing to please these austere black scholars.

His early life then was not that chamber of unremitting horrors which other Negro spokesmen assure us is the ordinary nurture of American Negroes. There were opportunities for genuine achievement: when he was thirteen, Farmer earned a four-year scholarship to college by winning a regional oratorical contest sponsored by the Improved Benevolent and Protective Order of Elks of the World, the Negro Elks. He had survived local and state contests. And there were chances for contact with the wider culture: in 1936 Farmer joined the National Council of Methodist youth and was soon elected vice-chairman of the national organization. Like most of the young people in the organization Farmer was hypnotized by the Social Gospel and began dreaming of creating a Kingdom of God on Earth. It was at this time too that he became seriously interested in pacifism. Farmer once described to me his feelings at this time: "It was my first opportunity to rub shoulders with people of all races from all over the country, in a thoroughly interracial setting. And to meet the best young minds in the country from some of the best schools. And I found that while there were gaps in my education, when it came to an intellectual discussion, I could hold my own and I developed more confidence as a result."

Teachers populate his memories more often than policemen. Teachers like Melvin B. Tolson, the celebrated poet, who forced him to think analytically and "feel" intelligently; and V. F. Calverton, the Marxist literary critic, who came to Wiley as a visiting lecturer, befriended Farmer, and became a formative influence in his development in the next few years. Books were as crucial to his development as billy clubs, books by Gandhi, Shridharani, Rauschenbusch, Weber.

"Discrimination," Farmer once said, "increased my determination to do something about inferiority feelings. I felt handicapped, but I never doubted my abilities." Of course, there was injustice too, and even the most fleeting experience of it caused a bitter taste which never quite left the senses. He was three and a half, walking home with his mother from shopping, down a dusty red road in Mississippi, holding tight to her finger. They passed a drugstore and he asked if they could stop for a Coke. She said they couldn't. "Why?" he asked, noting that another little boy had entered the store and was now sipping a Coke. "He can, and we can't." Again, "Why?" "Because he's white." "What am I then?" "You're not." Many years later Farmer was not sure if this little scene, which tormented his sleep, had actually happened. His mother confirmed the memory and added straight out that when they got home that day she had thrown herself across the bed and wept.

After graduating from Wiley, Farmer went to Howard to study theology, presumably to enter the ministry. He received his Bachelor of Divinity in 1941, but refused ordination. "I didn't see how I could honestly preach the Gospel

of Christ in a church that practiced discrimination." In that
year he returned to the South, for the first time in three
years, and for the first time in his life, really, saw how thoroughly racism blights our land.

It is precisely because his soul was *not* formed by racist
segregation that he had the humanity and strength to resent
it and the personal resources to fight it. I do not think we
do the truth about our racist culture any service by pro-
claiming that the American Negro is the utter and total
victim of racism. Racism can explain the anger, but what
can explain the humanity?

What followed next in Farmer's life he himself discusses
in Chapter 3. To summarize briefly here: From 1941 to
1945 he was race relations secretary of the pacifist Fellowship of Reconciliation, and it was in that capacity that he
helped found CORE in 1942 and began to lay the theoretical groundwork for the non-violent, direct-action mass
movement he was to lead. From 1946 he participated in the
Southern organizing drive of the Upholsterer's International
Union. From 1950 to 1954 he was youth secretary for the
League for Industrial Democracy, a democratic-socialist
group, and then he returned to union work with the State,
County, and Municipal Employees Union, representing that
group in 1958 on a five-member union delegation which
visited fifteen African countries. Throughout this period he
remained active in CORE as a volunteer. In 1959, at Roy
Wilkins' invitation, he joined the NAACP staff, eventually
becoming Program Director. And in 1961 he became
CORE's National Director.

Mrs. Farmer is the former Lula Peterson, whom he met
at a CORE meeting in 1945. They have two young daughters, Tami Lynn and Abbey Lee. Mrs. Farmer is white, and
her husband says that that doesn't occur to him except
when people ask him about it.

There is one other development in James Farmer's life which deserves note. In the past few years—it is difficult to date its beginning precisely—Farmer has noted in himself an enlarging and ever more enriching sense of racial pride. This is a significant turn in the story of a man who once was an aggressively color-blind idealist. But on this further comment is unnecessary, for the entire book is itself commentary.

Jacob Cohen
WALTHAM, MASSACHUSETTS
JULY, 1965

1

A
SOUTHERN TALE

I WOULD like to begin with the story of an experience I had in the summer of 1963 in Plaquemine, Louisiana. It is, I believe, a tale of the modern South which could be told, with only the details altered, by thousands of civil rights workers in Selma, in Bogalusa, in Meridian. And it can be an instructive introduction to our reflections on the state of freedom in this land.

Until recently Plaquemine was a little town drowsing on the banks of the Mississippi. That difficult balance of social repression with personal benevolence, common to the South, preserved peace and order and a somewhat illusory sense of well-being. The Negroes, at least with one part of their minds, regarded the white people as "good white folks." The whites in turn, with the same part of their minds, thought of the Negroes as jovial and good-natured, content with their lot. They felt honestly surprised when the Negroes began to agitate for the vote.

In the summer of 1963, while many prepared for the famed March on Washington, CORE launched one of its early voter-registration drives in a number of parishes in Louisiana, including Iberville Parish and its principal city of Plaquemine.* Actually there are few Negroes in Plaquemine proper, because the city boundaries have been deliberately engineered to exclude them. The city is horseshoe-shaped, surrounding a Negro community in its midst but refusing to incorporate it legally. As a result this Negro community is deprived of all municipal benefits: the roads are unpaved, sewage runs along the streets in open gutters. Understandably a number of people in this utterly disfranchised Negro community showed interest in the registration drive. A few local professional people— the only Negro doctor in the parish, the Negro school principal—at last were coming forward to assume leadership, despite the jeopardy in which such activity placed their jobs.

As a further stimulus to the drive our field secretary from New Orleans, Ronnie Moore, had asked me, in my capacity as National Director (outside agitator number one), to put in an appearance in the area. So I went down to Plaquemine toward the end of August on the first day of what I innocently assumed would be a routine three-day trip. We staged a protest march into town after my speech. When the march was over, all the leaders, myself included, were arrested and taken off to jail in nearby Donaldsonville (which hospitably offered us its facilities in lieu of the already overcrowded Plaquemine jail).

We stayed in jail for a week and a half. As a result, I missed the March on Washington. The timing was unfortu-

---

* The city of Plaquemine is not to be confused with Plaquemines Parish, the county presided over by the savagely segregationist political boss, Judge Leander Perez.

nate, but I felt that I really had no choice. Having cast my lot with the people of Plaquemine, I could not simply pull rank and walk out. Moreover, this was my opportunity to reaffirm publicly the insight that CORE had gained during the Freedom Rides of the previous year—that filling the jails could serve as a useful instrument of persuasion. So I sent a message to Washington, which was read by Attorney Floyd B. McKissick, CORE's national chairman, and remained in jail until all the local demonstrators were out. When we came out, the spirit of militancy was spreading in Plaquemine, and two days later a group of young people organized another demonstration, protesting segregation in public places as well as exclusion from the city. This time, however, the marchers did not even get into town. The chief of police stopped them halfway, arrested the leaders, and held the rest of the marchers where they were until state troopers arrived. The troopers came on horseback, riding like cowboys, and they charged into the crowd of boys and girls as if they were rounding up a herd of stampeding cattle. They were armed with billy clubs and cattle prods, which they used mercilessly. Many of the youngsters who fell under the blows were trampled by the horses. (The children of Selma, whose suffering at the hands of police appalled the nation two years later, were but a part of a spiritual community of brave Southern youngsters like these who for years have been deprived of national attention by inadequate press coverage.)

This gratuitous savagery inflicted upon their children immediately aroused the adults to a pitch of militancy much more intense than anything the organizational effort had been able to achieve. The ministers, who had previously hung back, united for the first time. (Only one minister, the Rev. Jetson Davis, had been active in the movement. It was his Plymouth Rock Baptist Church to which

the injured boys and girls had fled for comfort and medical assistance.) Apathy or fear or whatever had caused
their reluctance dissolved in outrage. The next morning,
Sunday, every minister in the Negro quarter preached a
sermon extolling freedom and condemning police brutality.
After church, according to agreement, they led their con-
gregations to Reverend Davis' church and organized a
massive march in protest against the rout of the previous
day. As the time approached for the march to begin, some
of the ministers began to waver. One of them hesitated on
his way to the front of the line. "Where's my wife?" he
said, looking around fearfully. "I don't see my wife. I think
I'd better just go on home." His wife was standing right
behind him. "Man," she said, "if you don't get up there in
the front of that line, you ain't got no wife."

He marched, all right, but his presence could not alter
the course of events. This time when the troopers inter-
cepted the marchers there was nothing impromptu about
the confrontation. They did not even come on horseback;
they came in patrol cars and the horses arrived in vans.
The troopers mounted their horses and assembled their
weapons as if the crowd of unarmed men and women before them were an opposing army; they charged into the
mass as they had done the day before, flailing with billy
clubs and stabbing with cattle prods. "Get up, nigger!"
one would shout, poking a man with an electric prod and
beating him to the ground with a club. "Run, nigger, run!"

I was waiting at the Plymouth Rock Church. I watched
the Negroes come running back, those who could run,
bleeding, hysterical, faint, some of the stronger ones carrying the injured. The nurse started to bandage the wounds
and the rest of us began to sing "We Shall Overcome"; but
the troopers rode roaring through the streets right up to

the door of the church. The Freedom Rock Church, we call it now. They dismounted and broke into the church, yelling and hurling tear gas bombs in front of them—bomb after bomb, poisoning the air. The gas masks protecting the troopers' faces transformed them into monsters as they stood and watched our people growing more and more frantic, screaming with pain and terror, trampling on one another in their frenzied efforts to escape through the back door to the parsonage behind the church. When the people had finally escaped, the troopers set about destroying the empty church. They knocked out the windows, overturned the benches, laid waste everything they could reach, and flooded the gutted building with high-pressure hoses until Bibles and hymnals floated in the aisles.

Then they attacked the parsonage to which we had fled. They sent tear gas bombs smashing through the windows, until all the windows were shattered and almost everyone inside was blinded and choking. The screaming was unbearable. I caught sight of Ronnie Moore administering mouth-to-mouth resuscitation to a young woman. People writhed on the floor, seeking oxygen. A few managed to push through the rear door into the parsonage yard, but the troopers, anticipating them, had ridden around to the back with more bombs to force them in again. And then bombs thrown into the parsonage forced them back out into the yard. All these men and women, who just that morning had resolutely banded together to reach out for freedom and dignity, were reduced now to running from torment to torment, helpless victims of a bitter game.

We tried to telephone for help, but the operators were not putting through any outgoing calls from the Negro section. Within the community, though, there was telephone service, and several calls got through to us in the parsonage. What had appeared to be random and mindless brutality proved to have had a mad purpose after all. It was a manhunt. Troopers were in the streets, kicking open doors, searching every house in the Negro community, overturning chairs and tables, looking under beds and in closets, yelling, "Come on out, Farmer, we know you're in there. Come on out, Farmer! We're going to get you." We could hear the screaming in the streets as the troopers on horseback resumed their sport with the cattle prods and billy clubs: "Get up, nigger! Run, nigger, run!" Holding their victims down with the cattle prod, they were saying, "We'll let you up, nigger, if you tell us where Farmer is." Two of our girls, hiding beneath the church, overheard one trooper saying to another, "When we catch that goddam nigger Farmer, we're gonna kill him."

Spiver Gordon, CORE field secretary in Plaquemine, who, people say, looks like me, told me later that he wandered out of the church into the street at this time. Sighting him, state troopers ran up shouting, "Here he is boys. We got Farmer. We got their m- - - - - f- - - - - - Jesus." A trooper beckoned to a crowd of hoodlums who were watching nearby, many holding chains, ropes, clubs. "What post we gonna hang him from?" said one. After Spiver convinced them he wasn't me, he took a good lacing for looking like me. An officer said, "He ain't Farmer. You've beat him enough. Put him in the car and arrest him."

There seemed no prospect of aid from any quarter. We were all suffering intensely from the tear gas, and the troopers kept us running with the bombs. In desperation I sent two people creeping through the grass from the parsonage to a funeral hall half a block away to ask for refuge. The owners of the hall agreed to shelter us (although I doubt that they knew what they were taking on). So we crawled on our bellies through the grass, in twos, threes, fours, making use of guerrilla tactics that some remembered from the war but none of us had ever learned as a technique of non-violent demonstration, until we reached our new sanctuary. Night had fallen by the time all three hundred of us were safely inside, jammed together like straws in a broom into two rooms and a hallway. The sound of screaming still echoed in the streets as the troopers beat down another Negro ("Run, nigger, run!") or invaded another house. The telephones were still useless.

Very shortly the troopers figured out where we were. One of them—a huge, raging, red-faced man—kicked open the back door of the funeral home and screamed, "Come on out, Farmer. We know you're in there. We're gonna get you." I was in the front room. I could look down the hallway, over all the heads, right into his face: it was flushed and dripping with sweat; his hair hung over his eyes, his mouth was twisted. Another trooper burst through the door to stand beside him. "Farmer! Come out!"

I had to give myself up. I felt like a modern Oedipus who, unaware, brought down a plague upon the city. In this hall, their lives endangered by my presence, were three hundred people, many of whom had never even seen me before that day. I began to make my way into the hall, thinking that I would ask to see the warrant for my arrest and demand to know the charges against me. But before I could take three steps the men around me grabbed me silently and pulled me back into the front room, whispering fiercely, "We're not going to let you go out there tonight. That's a lynch mob. You go out there tonight, you won't be alive tomorrow morning."

The trooper, meanwhile, had discovered a large Negro

in the back room. He shouted triumphantly: "Here he is, we got that nigger Farmer! Come on in, boys. We got him here."

"I'm not Farmer," the man said. A third trooper came in.

"That ain't Farmer," he said. "I know that nigger." They went through his identification papers. He wasn't Farmer.

Suddenly, to everyone's astonishment, a woman pushed her way through the crowd to the back room and confronted the troopers. It was the owner of the funeral home, a "Nervous Nellie," as they say, who had previously held herself apart from the movement. I can never know—she herself probably does not know—what inner revolution or what mysterious force generated in that crowded room plucked her from her caul of fear and thrust her forth to assert with such a dramatic and improbable gesture her new birth of freedom. A funeral hall is as good a place as any for a person to come to life, I suppose, and her action sparked a sympathetic impulse in everyone who watched as she planted herself in front of the first trooper and shook a finger in his face: "Do you have a search warrant to come into my place of business?"

The trooper stared down at her, confounded, and backed away. "No," he said.

"You're not coming into my place of business without a search warrant. I'm a taxpayer and a law-abiding citizen. I have a wake going on here."

I prayed inwardly that her valiant subterfuge would not prove to be a prophecy.

"This ain't no wake," the trooper said, looking around at the throng of angry, frightened people crushed together before him. "These people ain't at no wake."

"Well, you're not coming into my place of business without a search warrant." The accusing finger pushed him back to the door, where he muttered for a moment to his men outside, then turned and yelled, "All right. We got all the tear gas and all the guns. You ain't got nothin'. We'll give you just five minutes to get Farmer out here. Just five minutes, that's all." He slammed the door.

The door clanged in my ears like the door of a cell in death row. "I'll go out and face them," I said, but once again I was restrained. They would stick by me, these strangers insisted, even if they all had to die, but they would not let me out to be lynched. Someone standing near me pulled out a gun. "Mr. Farmer," he said, "if a trooper comes through that door, he'll be dead."

"If a trooper comes through that door, he may be dead," I conceded. "But what about the trooper behind him and all the ones behind that one? You'll only provoke them into shooting and we won't have a chance." Very reluctantly he allowed me to take the gun from him. It is hard for people to practice non-violence when they are looking death in the face. I wondered how many others were armed.

Then my own private thoughts engulfed me. Reverend Davis was leading a group in the Lord's Prayer; another group was singing "We Shall Overcome." I was certain I was going to die. What kind of death would it be? Would they mutilate me first? What does it feel like to die? Then I grew panicky about the insurance. Had I paid the last installment? How much was it? I couldn't remember. I couldn't remember anything about it. My wife and little girls—how would it be for them? Abbey was only two then—too young to remember; but Tami was four and a half, and very close to me—she would remember. Well, damn it, if I had to die, at least let the organization wring some use out of my death. I hoped the newspapers were out there. Plenty of them. With plenty of cameras.

I was terrified. The five minutes passed. Six. Seven. Eight. A knock at the front door. My lawyers from New Orleans, Lolis Elie and Robert Collins, identified themselves and squeezed in, breathless. New Orleans radio had broadcast the news that a manhunt was in progress in Plaquemine, and they had driven over immediately. The community, they said, was in a state of siege. Everywhere one looked one saw troopers, like an invading army. The two lawyers had crawled through the high grass to seek refuge in the graveyard, but when they got there the place came alive: there was a Negro behind every tombstone ("All find safety in the tomb," sang Yeats, in another context). Apparently everyone had counted on the dead to be more hospitable than the living. Apparently, also, everyone knew where I was, but no one was telling the white men. The troopers, it seemed, had been bluffing; they could not be wholly sure I was in the funeral home. It occurred to me that my physical safety, in some elusive way that had very little to do with me, had become a kind of transcendent symbol to all these people of the possibilities of freedom and personal dignity that existed for them. By protecting me, they were preserving their dreams. But did they understand, I wondered, that through their acts of courage during this desperate night they had taken the first great steps toward realizing these possibilities? Did they sense that they had gained at least some of that freedom for which they longed here, and now?

Just as the lawyers finished their story there was another knock at the door. For a moment I thought the troopers had come at last, until I remembered that troopers don't knock. The two men who entered were recently acquired friends from Plaquemine, and pretty rough characters in their own right: my neighbor from town, whom I shall call Fred, and Bill, a buddy of his, ex-Marines who, I knew, carried several guns in their car at all times. The troopers, they told me, had grown systematic. They had set up road-blocks on every street leading out of town. The men who had been waiting in the back had just driven off in the direction of the sheriff's office, presumably to get a search warrant. In short, if I did not get out right now, my life would not be worth a dime.

I told my lawyers to get in their car and try to drive out through the roadblocks. I thought the troopers might re-spect their identification as attorneys. If they got through, they were to call New York at once, call my wife and tell her I was all right, call Marvin Rich at CORE and have him get in touch with the FBI, call New Orleans and try to get some kind of federal protection. It was imperative that we make contact with the outside world.

Then Fred and Bill set forth their plan. The woman who owned the funeral home had two hearses. They would send the old one out as a decoy with just a driver, who would take it down the main streets, making sure it was spotted at every roadblock. If pursued, he would speed up. Meanwhile, we would try to escape in the second hearse which was waiting, its motor already running, in a garage which we could reach without going out of the house.

If there was something unsettling about the prospect of riding to safety in a hearse, it was nonetheless the logical conclusion to the macabre events of the day. And we could see no alternative. Fred and Bill led the way to the garage, forcing a passage through the sweating men and women who murmured phrases of encouragement and good wishes as we passed. I prayed that our departure would release

them from danger, marveling once more at the courage
and devotion shown by these strangers.

It was cool, briefly, in the garage, but the hearse was
hot and stuffy again. Ronnie Moore, Reverend Davis, and
I crawled into the back and crouched down—three rest-
less, nervous men huddled together in a space meant for
one motionless body. I thought I remembered that Huey
Long had once escaped from someone in a hearse, and for
a moment I almost felt like smiling. Someone climbed into
the driver's seat and we were off, speeding down the back
roads toward New Orleans. Fred and Bill, heavily armed
(although I did not know that at the time), followed us
in their car. We took a winding route with countless de-
tours over very rough country roads which the Negroes
knew more intimately than the whites. Although you can
drive from Plaquemine to New Orleans in less than two
hours by highway, it took us four and a half hours, despite
the fact that we were going very fast and did not stop at all.
Whenever a car approached we flattened out on the floor
of the hearse until the road was clear again. Our grim des-
tination was another funeral home; our only protection
was blackness, a color which had never before promised
immunity to Negroes in the South. At times during that
wild ride I thought I was already dead. I don't know what
the others thought. But when at last we climbed out of the
hearse into the hot New Orleans night, we were, by the
grace of God and the extraordinary courage of many ordinary men, still very much alive. And not yet entirely out
of danger.

When we finally got in touch with the New Orleans
CORE, we discovered that our story was already out. The
two lawyers had passed the roadblocks and called the authorities in New Orleans, and the press had picked up the
news immediately. They had also called my wife, before

she had heard anything, to tell her not to worry: "Jim's all right."

"Oh," said Lula. "Why shouldn't he be?"

"There was a little trouble down in Plaquemine, but there's nothing to worry about now. He's out of danger." Whereupon Lula turned on the television set and learned that there was a house-to-house search reportedly going on in Plaquemine, Louisiana, for CORE National Director, James Farmer . . . and, a little later, that James Farmer was reported missing in Plaquemine, Louisiana. She told me later that she turned off the news broadcast and took the children outside where the voices they would hear were less ominous. Shortly afterward, when she went to call the press to try to find out more, she found they were already waiting for her at the house.

In New York, though, they never carried the complete story. The next morning I held a press conference at the CORE headquarters in New Orleans. Newspaper and TV reporters carefully took down all the details, but what they wrote never got farther than New Orleans. But then the list of stories that the newspapers have overlooked in the South and elsewhere is endless.

A trial was scheduled for me the next day in Plaquemine. I was not exactly eager to return but I announced at the press conference that I intended to appear at the appointed time to be served with the warrant for my arrest and to hear the charges, whatever they might be. The FBI sent a man to New York to find out the details from our national office. Our people told him I was going back into Plaquemine the next day and asked if the FBI could guarantee my safety; our attorney, Lolis Elie, called the FBI regional office in New Orleans with the same request. To both requests, the response was the same: the FBI was an investigatory agency, not a protection agency; they could not guarantee my life. However, since the situation was an extraordinary one, they would see what they could do.

With this ambiguous support, Ronnie Moore, Reverend Davis, and I returned somewhat nervously to Plaquemine the next morning. The city police were waiting for us; as soon as we drove into town we saw a policeman in a squad car in front of us announce our arrival into his radio. To our relief FBI agents were everywhere, questioning people in the Negro section, the white section, and around the courthouse. Two agents came over to me as soon as I walked into the courtroom. But as it turned out the troopers had no warrant for my arrest, no charges against me. Nor could we take any action against them, for their name plates and badge numbers had been taped over during the manhunt. In fact, we learned that many of the men who had been riding that night were not even regular troopers: they were ordinary citizens deputized for the occasion.

The drama of Plaquemine ended there, but its consequences are still alive. A new Negro community grew out of that terrible night, aroused, unified, determined to act. When the parish sheriff was up for re-election, the Negro leaders arranged a meeting with his white opponent to ask him about his platform. There was no question of his being an integrationist, of course, but they wanted to know how he stood on the issue of police brutality. Quite emphatically he replied that he was against it, that he had no use for tear gas, billy clubs, or cattle prods, that he had felt that way all his life, and that if he was elected sheriff he would "put a stop to all this nonsense." Just a few days before the election, in a carefully timed maneuver, Reverend Davis, who was also running, withdrew and threw all his votes to this man. He won, too, by a margin so slim there could be no doubt that he owed his victory to the Negro vote. Since assuming office, moreover, he has kept his word on the question of police brutality and has appointed several Negro deputy sheriffs. He is still an uncompromising segregationist: I want to stress that point. Militant non-violence has not reached his heart, nor is it likely to. But the election of this segregationist sheriff with his policy of decency suggests an important truth which CORE has slowly learned to accept: In the arena of political and social events, what men feel and believe matters much less than what, under various kinds of external pressures, they can be made to *do*. The Negro vote also defeated Jumonville, Iberville's parish state representative and a protégé of Leander Perez, who was alleged by local Negroes to be one of the men deputized to ride that night. Jumonville reportedly accosted one of the Negro leaders after the election with the friendly recommendation that the next time they had a demonstration they had better let him know, because he intended to join them.

But if the hearts of hostile Southerners are likely to be out of reach, the hearts of the men and women involved in the movement are very much within our province. CORE, from its earliest beginnings, has wanted to involve the people themselves, individually, personally, in the struggle for their own freedom. Not simply because it was clear that no one else was going to confer liberty upon them, but because in the very act of working for the impersonal cause of racial freedom, a man experiences, almost like grace, a large measure of private freedom. Or call it a new comprehension of his own identity, an intuition of the expanding boundaries of his self, which, if not the same thing as freedom, is its radical source. This is what happened in Plaquemine to the owner of the funeral home, to the men who kept silence in the graveyard, to the men and women who stood between me and the lynch mob. Gradually, during the course of those two violent days, they made the decision to act instead of being acted upon. The group of people who assembled on Sunday morning were in large part reacting viscerally to the police brutality of the previous day; but the same people that evening, who, although packed together in the funeral hall, refused to be victimized any longer by the troopers, had been transformed into a community of men, capable, despite the severest limitations, of free and even heroic acts. Their subsequent activity at the polls and in initiating a school boycott suggests that this kind of freedom, though essentially personal, will inevitably lead to social action, and that freedom once won is not readily surrendered.

There are also more somber lessons to be drawn from the events at Plaquemine, darker reflections on the future of the movement. CORE is a mass movement now and no longer commands the dedicated allegiance it once did to the principles of non-violence. What will happen when the Negroes, their self-awareness heightened, experience brutality or repression? What do Negroes and whites really see when they look at each other now that the mists of sleep have been brushed aside? Vision is a terrifying gift. All the energy that has been released is in the service of this vision, and it carries with it a payload of violence.

In the funeral hall in Plaquemine, I overheard two people standing by a window, in a conversation that went something like this:

"Did you see who was ridin' one of those horses? Adams' son!"

"No! You're wrong, they're good white people. Adams has been a friend of our family as long as we've been here. I practically brought his son up."

"Just look at him there, riding one of those horses, with a cattle prod in his hand."

And then a third person said something heard more and

more from Negroes in Plaquemine: "The only good white man is a dead one."

The humiliation and fury that a man feels when he has been brutally treated are rendered insupportably bitter if he discovers that he has also been betrayed. You may say that the Negroes will not be susceptible to betrayal much longer, for they are rapidly flinging aside all their illusions about the good will of the white man. But to insure oneself unequivocally against betrayal, one must discard more than illusions; one must also abandon any prospect of trust, or faith, in the white man. And many Negroes are hardening their hearts in this way. They have cast off their outgrown shells, like the mollusks on the beach, and are growing new, more formidable armor which protects them not only from illusion but from conciliation and compromise as well, and in very extreme cases from reason and self-control. On another occasion, I spoke at a rally in West Feliciana Parish which was attended by a number of young Negro men from neighboring Plaquemine. After the meeting I discovered that they all had guns in their cars; they had vowed that nothing was going to happen to Mr. Farmer this time. As we stood outside the church where our meeting had taken place, the sheriff of the parish and a carload of rednecks drove slowly back and forth past the church, then parked on the other side of the street and stared, tauntingly. The young men with me stood with their arms folded, staring back. Tension stretched like a wire across the street. No fight broke out that night, but if it had, the Negroes would have grabbed for their guns. And what will prevent that fight the next time, or the time after that?

Lest you dismiss young boys of this kind as the "hoodlum" element, or the armed ex-Marines in Plaquemine as the "rougher" element, let me make it clear that most Ne-

groes in the South own, or have access to, guns. On the
night of the violence in Plaquemine the Negro school
principal's mentally retarded son wandered into the street
by himself. When his mother realized that he was gone, she
became hysterical and grabbed a gun and ran wildly out
into the night looking for troopers. Fortunately, someone
in her family found her before she found the troopers and
dragged her back to the house. But she was ready to shoot.
And the seventy-year-old woman at a rally in Canton,
Mississippi, who opened her pocketbook to look for something and pulled out a pistol—she was ready to shoot, too.
And in Bogalusa, Louisiana, early in 1965, when an already
tense racial situation was aggravated by the murder of one
of two Negroes on the parish police force—a man who had
been hired through the efforts of civil rights workers—
the Negroes responded by organizing their own civilian
defense force, which they call the Deacons. The Deacons
constitute a fully armed and trained militia, holding regular
drills, and are prepared to respond with organized violence
to any attack upon the Negro community. When I went
down to speak in Bogalusa in June, my personal safety was
in the hands of the FBI *and* the Deacons.* The CORE people working in Bogalusa have interested the Deacons in a
wider program of civil rights, but we haven't persuaded them
to give up their arms.

I have often quoted Gandhi to the effect that I would
much prefer to see a man resist evil with violence than fail
to resist evil out of fear. We grope, of course, for the middle ground, on which evil will be resisted yet violence will
be avoided. CORE and the other non-violent organizations have taken their stand on this middle ground, but the
area of their effectiveness seems to be rapidly dwindling.

* The State Police, the same agency that had sought my blood in
Plaquemine, also provided protection.

One reason is that the young Negroes are more impatient than the old. Having been less encumbered from the beginning with illusions, they measure progress with a sterner eye. Why should they believe time to be on their side? But another, more difficult reason has to do with the fact that the time it takes for fear to explode into violence is even briefer than the behavior of today's Negroes might indicate. The fear that for so many years bound the Negro to passive acquiescence in his degradation has evaporated. The danger is that in its place a spring of resentment and fury will boil up which can know no expression short of violence.

Luckily the citizens of Plaquemine and Bogalusa, black and white, and the citizens of the rest of the Deep South need not be left to their own devices. However stubbornly these sovereign states may deny it, they are part of one nation, and the resources of this nation—economic, political, moral, and when necessary, military—can and must be used to cure the South of its vicious self-absorption. There are statutes in the U. S. Code forbidding the exclusion of jurors on the grounds of race or color and declaring that jury rolls must be representative of the general population in the areas from which the rolls are drawn. When the federal government enforces these statutes, as it is legally obliged to do, then justice for Negroes in states like Mississippi, Alabama, and Louisiana can become a reality. If the federal government were to withdraw its subsidies from the school lunch programs, the farm programs, the state unemployment services, hospital and highway construction programs, in all cases where these funds are racially administered or serve to promote segregation, then the poorer Southern states would be forced to change their ways. After all, the civil rights workers in the South are only doing the job which the federal government ought to be doing for itself: insuring for all citizens the enjoyment of their Constitutional rights.

No one is so ignorant of the South as these Southerners who inveigh against "outside agitators with no understanding of local problems." For they actually suppose that they can restore yesterday *in toto* without soaking their soil in blood. Can they not understand that when we demand "massive federal presence" in the South, we ask not only a show of power to secure our Constitutional rights but a reassertion of a just order which we feel alone will preserve the peace for all Southerners? Will they not see that in the example and witness of the black people of the South they are permitted to glimpse the deepest and purest spirit of this nation and that merely by emulating it they can end the moral estrangement which torments them so? We are not only for ourselves.

2

"... BUT WHEN WILL THE WILL THE DEMONSTRATIONS END?"

"... B U T when will the demonstrations end?" The perpetual question. And a serious question. Actually it is several questions, for the meaning of the question differs, depending upon who asks it.

Coming from those whose dominant consideration is peace—public peace and peace of mind—the question means: "When are you going to stop tempting violence and rioting?" Some put it more strongly: "When are you going to stop *sponsoring* violence?" Assumed is the necessary connection between demonstration and violence.

Others say, "I don't mind professionally organized, skillful demonstrations, with specific and limited objectives; it is these amateurish, exhibitionistic demonstrations that I deplore. What good do they accomplish, besides satisfying egos?" And the assumption here, of course, is that professionals are invariably preferable to amateurs and that, by itself, the satisfaction of black egos is somehow an unworthy accomplishment.

"Isn't the patience of the white majority wearing thin? Why nourish the displeasure of 90 per cent of the population with provocative demonstrations? Remember, you need allies." And the assumption of these Cassandras of the backlash is that freedom and equality are, in the last analysis, wholly gifts in the white man's power to bestow.

And then the question we shall face again and again in this book: "Even granting that there was a time when demonstrations were useful, can we not, now that Negro civil rights are nearly secure, turn to more familiar techniques of political participation and press for sorely needed economic reforms?" And the assumptions of these questioners, who include some of the most formidable figures in the civil rights movement, are both that Negro rights are secure and that demonstrations will be ineffective in gaining economic reform.

These are appropriate questions to put to a CORE spokesman, for I believe that CORE, more than any other civil rights organization, has been responsible, in the quarter century since it was founded, for bringing the Negro's century-long struggle for freedom and equality into the streets.* Certainly in the public's mind we are most closely identified with demonstrations and other forms of direct action. Demonstration has been our stock in trade, and while for some time we have been engaged in a program reaching beyond and behind demonstrations,† we still feel they have an important role. When efforts are afoot to discredit the traditions of direct action and dismantle weapons we shall need time and again in the future, it is CORE's job to speak up.

So I shall speak to these questioners and their questions.

* See Chapter 3.
† See Chapter 7.

I. OF DEMONSTRATIONS AND RIOTS

I must insist that a demonstration is not a riot. On the contrary, rather than leading to riots, demonstrations tend to help prevent them by providing an alternative outlet for frustrations. In New York City in the summer of 1963, for example, anger and frustration were just as high as they were to be in the riotous summer of 1964. But in 1963 we had hundreds of mass demonstrations aimed at pointing up discrimination in the building trades. Many unemployed youths, aimlessly prowling in the streets, joined the demonstrations—picketing, climbing cranes, blocking bulldozers; they did not have to resort to throwing bottles and bricks, and they didn't. But in the summer of 1964 for many reasons there were few demonstrations, and the riots came about. I don't mean to imply that there is a direct cause-and-effect relationship between organized protest and relative public peace, but certainly there is some relationship. We have seen it countless times, in the South as well as the North. Walking the streets in Harlem during the riots, I saw more clearly than I have ever before how young men who feel that nothing is being done about grievances so deep they can barely articulate them, will finally spring to violence.

How does a riot happen? A detailed look at the July, 1964, events in Harlem may be instructive. On July 16, an off-duty police lieutenant named Thomas Gilligan shot and killed a slight, fifteen-year-old Negro, Jimmy Powell. Powell was one of several hundred students, mainly Negro and Puerto Rican, attending summer school in Yorkville—a largely white area near Harlem. The students—many of whom had witnessed the shooting—were furious, many of them literally choking with rage at such wanton injustice. Impromptu leaders advised their fellow students to tear up the neighborhoods. On Friday, July 17, CORE workers organized hundreds of Powell's schoolmates in a protest march from the school to the nearest precinct house, where they demanded Gilligan's suspension and a civilian investigation. That demonstration, all agree, was a model of peaceful protest and was thoroughly successful in sublimating the anger of the youngsters.

Meanwhile parts of Harlem began to seethe. "We must *do* something," people said. I firmly believe that if Harlemites had been better trained in legitimate mass demonstrations (demonstrating *is* doing something)—and if the police had not acted so unwisely—the Harlem riots could have been averted. Rioting and looting broke out in the evening of July 18.* Three local chapters of CORE— Downtown, East River, and South Jamaica—had held a protest meeting that night at 7 P.M. on 125th Street and Seventh Avenue. It was a small meeting, attended by perhaps two hundred people. After the meeting about a hundred people marched to the precinct station at 123rd Street. CORE leaders decided to go along in order to maintain the discipline of a demonstration. At the precinct house the marchers demanded Gilligan's suspension; the officer in charge, Inspector Thomas V. Prendergast, shouting through a bull horn, informed the crowd that he had just spoken to Police Commissioner Michael Murphy, who would come to Harlem to address the crowd. The CORE leaders began to talk to the gathering crowd, explaining that they were waiting for Murphy and maintaining rea-

---

* People often fail to distinguish between rioting and looting. In some rudimentary form, rioters are protesting; looters will appear whenever there is chaos and confusion (there was widespread looting in Alaska at the time of an earthquake). In my opinion, there was more looting during the riots than rioting. And a failure to see that gave the impression that the rioting was far more widespread than it was.

sonable order. At this point the demonstration was well contained, little different from many our CORE people had seen. Individuals hurled abuse at the police, but big talk from crowds of this kind is common. The police are used to it. Then, surprisingly, at about 7:20, a truck came, carrying police barricades. A fight broke out between a policeman and a bystander while the barricades were being erected. At that, Inspector Prendergast, who was in charge, took the astounding action of arresting CORE leaders. He shouted: "I've had enough of this. Get them niggers. Arrest all of them."* Suicidal words in Harlem. It was then that the crowd went crazy and began throwing bottles and bricks. Suddenly policemen were pouring out of the station, buckling on their holsters. They began pushing the crowd back. A bus with forty-eight members of the Tactical Patrol Force—the shock troops—came rolling up. *"Charge!"* they shouted, as if in some movie Western.

The police could not have acted more foolishly that evening had they tried, but then clearly they were thirsting for action. Policemen feel the heat too. Prendergast, who was soon to be promoted, lost his head. And those who feel that the police behavior had no racist overtones should ponder the following account, by Ted Poston of the *New York Post,* of how the police handle *white* rioters:

> At the same time that hundreds of white helmeted police were firing volleys of bullets over the heads of Harlem rioters and striking out, sometimes indiscriminately with night sticks, police were putting down another riot around Police Headquarters itself where 1,000 white youths— mainly Italian—were attacking some 300 CORE pickets who were peacefully demonstrating. . . . Frustrated in

---

* I did not hear this, but several CORE leaders, separately and independently, reported the same words. I believe them.

their efforts to get at the CORE demonstrators, the white rioters in turn attacked the police, knocking one inspector half unconscious with a hurled stone and injuring several others. Yet here not one police billy club was raised nor one pistol unsheathed. Yet even as his inspector was being rushed to a nearby hospital, blood streaming from his face, Commissioner Murphy, who witnessed the attack, told reporters: "There's no violence here. You can't equate *this* with what is happening in Harlem. . . ."

It was not without justification then that Harlem citizens felt, that hot July night, that the police (once again) were being especially brutal to them because they were black and that there was some connection between the motives of Gilligan in shooting young Powell and the excessive zeal with which policemen started beating their heads.

There have been other great riots in New York City— in March of 1935, in August of 1943—both immediately precipitated by the charge of police brutality—and they broke out without the presence of civil rights demonstrators. The most elementary review of riots in this city and others over the last century would instruct anyone willing to learn that a riot does not need an organized demonstration to trigger it. Nor do the people in the ghetto need civil rights workers to tell them they are disgruntled and that conditions are deplorable. Some people blamed the rioting on our predictions of a long hot summer; they forget that we coupled these predictions with specific demands. Again and again I asked Mayor Wagner for a civilian review board, and I'm sure that if Harlem had newly won that concession, the people would have been willing to await the findings of the board and no rioting would have occurred over the Gilligan affair. We could then have said: "We have a civilian review board at long last; let's give it a chance."

Again and again I urged that work brigades of unemployed youth be set up, to clean vacant lots, beautify the city, and under skilled supervision rehabilitate dreadful housing. Had it been done, youngsters instead of rioting would have been working, and they would have had money to spend.

In the year between Harlem and Watts the nation in general and Los Angeles in particular had learned little. Parker's police repeated and compounded the errors of Murphy's men. What began as a riot in Watts—and probably could have been contained by police restraint, as in Philadelphia a year earlier—soon became a full-fledged revolt, with bullet replying to bullet and targets pinpointed for fire and theft. Wanton disorder was fanned into tactical rebellion by the too eager pistols of Los Angeles police whose chief later chortled: "We're on top, and they're on the bottom."

The time bomb was loaded in Watts, and the now all but forgotten arrest incident which triggered it no more *caused* L.A.'s explosion than Gilligan's gun *caused* Harlem's. The causes lie deep in the morass of the city's failures—in housing and employment, and because of police abuse. Much worse, failure even to *see* that the problems existed in such abundance, and that Watts area people were people who had something to say and were worthy of being heard. Before the uprising Mayor Yorty was adamant in his refusal to permit representatives of the poor to sit on the city's anti-poverty board.

Rioting erupted in Harlem and Watts then, because the police behaved badly; because ghetto conditions manufacture social dynamite; because a legitimate case of police brutality, symbolic of a million other brutalities, came along to light the fuse; because of the reluctance of the cities' administrations to face much less begin to cope with palpable problems; and—most fundamental to the point of this discussion—because put-upon people could imagine no way to *do* something about their grievances except through violence.

One way to avert riots is to satisfy people that they can do something—not promise that things will be done, but satisfy them that they can do something without turning to self-defeating violence. One thing they can do is demonstrate.

They did just that in Chicago in the summer of 1965, and the predicted riots may thus have been averted. The objectives of eliminating de facto school segregation and getting rid of Superintendent Willis were not achieved, but masses were in motion: *something was being done*, and those who would be bomb throwers were thereby disarmed.

Mass demonstrations are an American ideal, the reflex actions of aggrieved men and groups—a technique of self-expression and political action as precious to a group of white parents protesting school integration as to Negroes protesting discrimination. It is common for Americans to read in their newspapers of strikes which tie up the nation's commerce and drain public coffers of millions of dollars. A businessman from Long Island will calmly peruse the headline and, unperturbed, turn to the sports page. In other words, the public permits the labor movement to dislocate the society occasionally, and this is part of a bargain we made with labor at a time when labor rioting and violence were common. Well, even as America overcame the violence of the early labor movement by establishing routine procedures for mass labor demonstrations, so must this country overcome racial violence which from time to time will break out in the ghetto by legitimatizing the techniques of mass action developed by the civil rights groups. It seems to me obvious that without demonstrations we will learn what violence and chaos really are. To inhibit mass demonstration is madness. And Negro leaders and others who encourage its inhibition are ill-advised.

I will not pretend that demonstrations are as disciplined as they once were. More than ever we have attracted the masses, undisciplined and angry. In Birmingham, 1963, it was the undisciplined mass which finally reacted with violent reprisals to the snapping dogs, the hoses, the cattle prods. And there were some who said consequently that mass demonstrations had gotten out of hand.

Obviously, no one should sponsor a demonstration whose only possible immediate consequence is mob violence. Every responsible leader agrees on that. Where they do not agree is whether in the face of greater mass participation— and its accompanying decrease of discipline—we should abandon all but the most polite demonstrations of protest. My own feeling is that if demonstrations are in danger of courting violence, the remedy is not to stop demonstrating but to perfect our ability to control the more undisciplined participants and to spread our teaching. At CORE we now encourage chapters to train a central core of people to monitor all demonstrations, spotting and isolating potential trouble. But we cannot turn back, and we will not renounce the masses, nor will we take the blame for the hatred our efforts reveal in the hearts of sheriffs and police commissioners.

II. ON THE "AMATEURISM" OF SOME DEMONSTRA-TIONS AND THE CHARGE THAT THEY SERVE ONLY TO SATISFY THE EGOS OF THE PARTICIPANTS

The trouble with the so-called professionals is that they turn the people into spectators. Let them watch, the professionals seem to say, while we, the specialists, the lawyers, the college men, the administrators, do the job for them. In CORE's direct-action philosophy the individual is directly and immediately involved; he speaks directly to the evil and often for the first time in his life experiences what it is to speak and be heard. One of the lessons I learned in Plaquemine is that too many lives are regenerated in the midst of direct action to return to the Age of the Experts.

Are we amateurs? We plead guilty as charged, and proudly. John Stuart Mill said, in *On Liberty,* that it is better to let people do things themselves, even if they do it less well, than to do it for them; his dictum has never been so demonstrably true as when applied to the civil rights movement. I will never say that I have approved of *all* CORE demonstrations. I felt, for example, that the proposed traffic tie-up at the opening of the New York World's Fair in April, 1964, was ill-advised and I helped organize a more effective—and highly successful—demonstration on the Fair grounds. But generally speaking, I have let our lovely amateurs have their heads.* I am sure that if

---

* Sometimes the amateurs save the day. In fact, if it weren't for some quick thinking by one at the World's Fair demonstration, the demonstration would never have come off. The plan of the authorities had been to stop me at the gate. Fortunately, some of our most dedicated young CORE members were already inside with walkie-talkies. One of them, with great ingenuity, tuned in on the Pinkertons' frequency and listened to their conversation. He was quite interested to hear the control tower speak to the Pinkertons: "Headquarters to Pi 1 and Pi 2, Headquarters to Pi 1 and Pi 2: Farmer is coming through the gate with a large group

the armchair experts could see the work and devotion which go into a CORE demonstration and could actively participate in an organized protest, they would not call a halt to an ineffective demonstration so quickly either. The sky will not fall if we make a few mistakes.

The government seems to have applied this lesson to its War on Poverty. The law says that the poor must be involved in planning for their own futures, and many leaders of the program have been quoted as saying that if we do not encourage impoverished communities to engage in direct action—picket lines, boycotts, rent strikes—all the money and loving care in the world will not succeed in providing them with a dignified life. I cannot stress this point too strongly. Our people must feel that they are shaping their own lives; that they have forced changes in the politics of the powerful. You cannot engineer freedom. A freed man is not yet free. I only hope the agencies—federal, state, and local—which are administering the anti-poverty program will have the courage of their rhetoric.

Even ego-satisfying demonstrations have some fringe benefits. Consider the problem of crime and juvenile delinquency in the ghetto. Both decreased drastically in Montgomery, Alabama, at the time of the bus boycott in 1956. Before the 1961 Freedom Rides, Jackson, Mississippi, had a shocking incidence of petty and violent crime of Negro against Negro. When the Freedom Buses came, the city united in support and the crime rate dropped precipitately. But perhaps the most dramatic example of the power of mass demonstrations to regenerate a Negro community occurred in 1963 in Cambridge, Maryland, where, in a move-

---

of people; stop him at the gate, do not let him enter." Our young man thought fast and decided he had to do something. Picking up the walkie-talkie, he said, "Headquarters to Pi 1 and Pi 2: disregard previous orders; let them through." It worked.

ment led by Gloria Richardson, arrests of Negroes for major crimes were cut by more than half.* Nor should we forget the success of the so-called Black Muslims in wiping out crime among their adherents. Whenever people are given hope and the technique to get the heel off their necks, crime will decline.

What the public must realize is that in a demonstration more things are happening, at more levels of human activity, than meets the eye. Demonstrations in the last few years have provided literally millions of Negroes with their first taste of self-determination and political self-expression. We might think of the demonstration as a rite of initiation through which the black man is mustered into the sacred order of freedom. It is also a rite the entire nation must undergo to exorcise the demons of racial hate. If in a spasm of emancipated exuberance these rites should cause inconvenience or violate the canons of cultivated good taste or trouble the dreams of some good-livers—I think it is forgivable. Enlightened people will understand that exuberance and occasional inconvenience are small prices to pay when a nation is undoing historic wrong. The very least the nation can do is give us room to demonstrate. That is only a small sacrifice, considering the debt.

In emphasizing the therapeutic value of demonstrations, I do not wish to suggest that they have ceased to be an effective tool and weapon. Few demonstrations are wholly

* This figure is taken from a report by a team of researchers from Howard University and The Johns Hopkins Hospital appearing in the March, 1965, *Archives of General Psychiatry*. The team studied three cities. In one, "a small town in a border state," which I take to be Cambridge, Maryland, arrests of Negroes for major crimes during the five warm months declined from seventy-three in 1961, before the local movement began, to thirty-one in 1963 at the height of demonstrations. In another city in the Deep South, which may be Atlanta, there was a 31-per-cent reduction in the rate of assault by Negroes upon other Negroes. In the third city, which I take to be Albany, Georgia, juvenile delinquency dropped markedly among gang members in the movement.

ineffective. Let us consider the *bête noire* of those complaining about "amateurish" demonstrations—the garbage-dump on the Triborough Bridge. The aim of that CORE demonstration was to inform a comfortable and complacent public about the reprehensible condition of two Harlem schools; the garbage we dumped was actually collected from trash and debris accumulated in those schools. The halls and dining rooms of the schools reeked. There had been a fire in one of them two weeks earlier; the charred debris had not been cleared. So we called the police and newspapers to tell them that we intended to scoop up heaps of filth and drop them on the bridge at midday, delaying traffic for about twenty minutes, and that we would distribute leaflets to drivers and the press explaining what we were doing and why. New York citizens should know what goes on inside the ghetto walls they skirt each day! Unfortunately, the press played up the garbage and ignored the leaflets. But CORE is not responsible for the failure of the news media to report its activities fully and objectively.

It will be asked: "What good is it to discomfort and anger people who themselves can do nothing about Harlem conditions? What except bad will can come of such provocations?" Often there is a threat concealed in the question. "Be careful, I'm getting angry. It will harm your cause if I am angry." Now, I am the last man to deprive someone of his anger; we have been demanding our own right to be angry for some time. We expect anger; but we expect honesty, too, and honesty would compel this angry man to admit that there is a contradiction in his position. On the one hand, he says that vague public sympathy and understanding will not help the cause (therefore we ought to demonstrate to persons immediately involved, not to the general public); on the other hand, he says that

vague public displeasure will harm the cause. If vague public displeasure can harm us, it follows that public sympathy with our plight can help. All of which means simply
that public policy is still determined in the context of public opinion.

No one of us at CORE ever claimed that the garbage-
dump alone would solve the education problem in New
York City or even a significant part of it—as if only those
demonstrations which single-handedly solved problems
were justified. What we do claim is that city officials will
not move to improve the quality and racial balance of the
schools until (a) both officials and the general public realize
that conditions are unconscionable, and (b) both realize
that they cannot skirt the issue without risking some dislocation. Teaching this is a long, cumulative process, and I
believe the Triborough affair played its role. In the spring
of 1965 the New York City Board of Education sketched
a far-reaching plan for upgrading and integrating the city
schools. Whether the plans will leave the drawing board
remains to be seen (we intend to use some persuasion), but
it is clear that in 1965 the city was closer to meeting its education problem than it had been a year earlier.

Actually, the cumulative impact of demonstrations far
and near is one of our most potent weapons. In the spring
and summer of 1962 CORE initiated a project called Freedom Highways. We would conduct demonstrations against
discrimination in major chain restaurants serving U.S.
highways. Howard Johnson immediately desegregated all
sixty-nine of its restaurants in Florida. Later in that year
we announced that we would begin a campaign against
discrimination in hiring at Sears, Roebuck and asked our
chapters throughout the country to investigate hiring policies of Sears, Roebuck stores in their localities. Some of
them telephoned the local manager: "This is CORE call-

ing. We want to come and talk to you about discrimination." "Don't bother," came several answers, "just send us a certain number of Negro sales personnel Monday morning." Our persuasive sort of negotiations convinced the First National Bank in Boston to hire several hundred Negroes. In California, twenty-six CORE chapters co-operated in persuading the Bank of America to hire thousands of Negroes and Mexican-Americans. In New York, a combination of economic boycott, picketing, and secondary pressure helped persuade the Sealtest Dairy to cease discrimination. When we finally sat down with them, our negotiations were very amicable.

What I am saying is that in these cases, and many others, we had to resolve not to retreat before serious negotiations were possible, and the cumulative impact of demonstrations and boycotts throughout the country helped us make our point. In a sense we are still drawing interest because of the Montgomery bus boycott and the more recent well-publicized demonstrations. Even a seemingly futile demonstration plays its part. Similarly, our government and the Russians established a record of determined militancy over ten years, each trying to convince the other that it really would use its H-bombs, before reasonable communication could begin. The total context of demonstrations makes private negotiation and political due process possible. News travels. Tomorrow some bank president in the Midwest threatened with direct action may hire Negroes because he doesn't want garbage dumped in his bank.

But perhaps the clearest example of the cumulative power of demonstrations to effect beneficial change is in the background to the Civil Rights Act of 1964. The late President Kennedy is fondly remembered by American Negroes, but it would be a disservice to historical accuracy

if we forgot how disappointed we were in the first two
and a half years of his tenure of office. Kennedy was
elected by Negro votes in 1960, and he had made several
promises in order to get those votes. One thing he promised was comprehensive civil rights legislation, and in his
famous "stroke of the pen" statement he promised to eliminate discrimination in federally assisted housing. After his
election Kennedy showed little inclination to keep those
promises. To be sure, the Justice Department was more
active in initiating voter registration suits in the South than
it had been under Eisenhower, but, presumably with the
concurrence of the Justice Department, Kennedy had appointed three known racists to the federal bench: William
Harold Cox of Mississippi (who described two hundred
voter applicants as "a bunch of niggers . . . chimpanzees
[who] ought to be in the movies rather than being registered to vote"); J. Robert Elliot of Georgia ("I don't
want those pinks, radicals, and black voters to outvote
those who are trying to preserve our segregation laws and
traditions"); and E. Gordon West of Louisiana (who
called the 1954 school desegregation decision "one of the
truly regrettable decisions of all time"). Racist federal
judges are perhaps the greatest obstacle to federally enforced equal rights in the South today.

Meanwhile, no stroke of the pen, though we had been
reliably informed that an executive order drawn up by his
staff to fulfill his promise had lain unsigned in his office
since 1961. So CORE people joined a campaign of the
National Committee Against Discrimination in Housing.
We figured JFK's pen had run dry, and we sent thousands of bottles of ink to the White House. As for the
Civil Rights Bill, it is clear that as late as five minutes before
Birmingham (May, 1963) the President intended to drop
civil rights legislation from the agenda of urgent business in

order to safeguard other parts of his legislative program.

But he had not reckoned on Birmingham and the outbreak of demonstrations which followed in its wake. By June 19, Kennedy sent Congress the most comprehensive civil rights bill in our history. "We face, therefore," he said, "a moral crisis as a country and a people."

But Birmingham alone did not convince Kennedy and the nation of what it had to do. It was Birmingham, as the culmination of nearly ten years of passionate and unceasing direct demonstration, which *finally* taught the nation that the "movement" would not stop short of the redress of those grievances. A hundred years of lobbying and legal suits did not achieve what the masses achieved in the streets with their demonstrations. That Lyndon Johnson has been far superior to his predecessor in the civil rights area is in part due to the fact that this superbly political man has perceived how significantly in the last ten years the Negro has altered the political realities a President must deal with.

It would be fatal to *announce* that we are going to drop direct demonstrations, for that would shatter the context for racial progress we have built in the past ten years. There is too much more to be done. If CORE had *announced* in advance to Sears, Roebuck that we were not going to have any demonstrations, then our campaign would have been infinitely more difficult *and ultimately*— since we will not retreat—*more violent*. Similarly, if we were to offer a vacation to the nation, if we were to let America remember what it was like with the pressure off, we might never get them back to work without resorting to even more extreme and more disruptive measures.

III. BUT WHAT CAN YOU DO WITHOUT WHITE ALLIES? YOU ARE BUT 10 PER CENT OF THE POPULATION. BEWARE THE BACKLASH.

The use of the backlash argument as a deterrent to demonstrations took classic expression in 1964, when the election campaigns were beginning. It would be well to confront this argument against that background.

In March, April, and May, George Wallace, racist governor of Alabama, had entered three Democratic Party primaries in the North and each time confounded even our professionally pessimistic predictions. At the same time, many whites in the North whom we assumed to be sympathetic or at least usefully passive were expressing impatience with the direct methods the movement had used so dramatically and successfully in recent years. "What more do they want? They got the Civil Rights Act. They're pushing too hard!" More ominously, anti-Negro *sentiment* was hardening into concrete actions as Parents and Taxpayers Associations and neighborhood protection societies and anti-fair housing committees organized to fight desegregation. As we read letters in the CORE office and talked to people around the nation, it often seemed that good white folk had taken leave of their senses. Every subway incident was interpreted as a civil rights demonstration. Often I was challenged by a question which could be considered rational only if one assumed that Roy Wilkins, Martin Luther King, John Lewis, and I met each midnight, in a huge room filled with maps and charts, and simply by placing a pin in the map at a point, induced some poor ghetto victim to go berserk. I was even asked once why I couldn't keep my people quiet in the Congo. And *we* are supposed to believe in black magic! And then of course a Negro youngster was shot down by a trigger-happy cop and there were riots in Harlem, Rochester, Philadelphia, and Jersey City. And "responsible people" began deploring our "strike-back tactics." Early in July, Goldwater was nominated and we all agreed his election would be calamitous, not so much, perhaps, because of what he would do as for what his election would mean about the temper of the times.

On Monday, July 25, I received a telegram from Roy Wilkins, Executive Secretary of the NAACP, urging me to attend a meeting at his office to discuss tactics and strategy in the light of recent developments, adding that he was sure I was opposed to Goldwater and would not wish to do anything that would enhance his chances of election or hurt the civil rights movement. I couldn't disagree.

On July 29 I found myself in what the press later termed a "summit meeting" convened to proclaim a moratorium of all civil rights demonstrations until election day. Others present were Wilkins, Whitney Young (Urban League); Martin Luther King (Southern Christian Leadership Conference); John Lewis (SNCC); Jack Greenberg (NAACP Legal Defense and Education Fund, Inc.); A. Philip Randolph, the elder statesman of the movement; and Bayard Rustin, organizer of the March on Washington.

The key paragraph in the statement privately presented to this group for discussion read: "We therefore propose and call upon our members to observe a moratorium of all mass marches, picketing, and demonstrations until after Election Day, next November 3." This was later amended for public presentation to read: ". . . a broad curtailment, if not total moratorium of all mass marches, etc." But to the press and general public, never patient with fine distinctions, the moratorium was blanket, and I think they captured, for once, the principal impulse of the event.

The *New York Daily News*, in an unusual show of insight, applauded the move and urged the civil rights leaders to follow the logic of their statement and make the moratorium permanent. After all, if a cessation of mass agitation would help elect Johnson now, why not begin the 1968 campaign the day after the election. One cannot be too prudent in politics.

The reasoning behind the moratorium was clear: Goldwater had to be defeated; we must not antagonize whites into voting for him; the "strike-back" philosophy gains only enemies and since we cannot achieve our goals if the entrenched and powerful 90 per cent oppose us, our prime policy must be "winning friends and influencing people among the white majority." Therefore, we must halt "ego-satisfying" demonstrations and emphasize voter registration. A grateful Democratic Party will be useful.*

At CORE we agreed that Goldwater should be defeated, and we agreed, too, that voter registration was important and that we should add political action to our program of direct action. And we agreed that we could not achieve our goals if the entrenched and powerful 90 per cent opposed us (that isn't exactly a controversial statement), but we did not agree that demonstrations should end because of white sentiment, nor did we agree that a handful of leaders should *announce* our intention and willingness to end demonstrations. So CORE rejected the moratorium, as did SNCC. And our reasons are as sound today, when applied to the backlash argument, as they were in 1964.

First, I must challenge the factual basis of the moratorium decision. It was not true in 1964 and it is not true now

* The quotes in this paragraph are from Mr. Wilkins' article explaining the moratorium to readers of the *New York Times Magazine*, August 16, 1964.

that we are in danger of causing 90 per cent of the population to array itself against us. Outside the South "whiteness" is not the principle upon which most non-blacks vote and act, and even in the South it is not the only political banner. In a sense the moratorium-mongers are using a Muslim-like argument—invoking the specter of racial war—to support their strategy. If the movement *could* suddenly lose the support of its allies in organized labor, in the church, in the intellectual community, in the various liberal organizations, in the Democratic and Republican parties, simply because it insists on being honest to itself and its tasks, then it never had those friends to begin with. Why oppose Goldwater, if things are in this state, if he'll win eventually anyway? Not that everything we do will please our friends. At times we will distress them, they will growl imperiously. And at times they will be right and change our minds. But that they will suddenly array themselves against us—white against black—is unlikely. I believe we should ally ourselves with white groups; I believe we are allied and I believe the alliance is firm enough to withstand some independence in its parties.

With the advantage of hindsight I might add that the backlash failed to snap for Goldwater and that mid-1965 polls showed, after Selma and Bogalusa, that the nation supported Congress' efforts to pass a tough voting bill.*

By acceding to the backlash, we only convince hostile white groups that they can intimidate us into inaction by threatening to vaunt their own displeasure. When would be the next time a moratorium would be demanded, this time with the added argument: "You did it in '64 and it worked; Goldwater was defeated. Why not do it now"?

* At writing, the bill seems to be weaker than we had hoped it would be. A section prohibiting poll taxes in state and local elections—as they have been banned in federal elections—was deleted.

Each concession makes the next one harder to avert. Worse still, backlashism trains black men to pin their sense of priorities to the tail of current white feelings or, more precisely, to what are perceived to be current white feelings. This not only corrupts thought, it dams up healthy and manly instincts. Soon we see white opposition where there is none; even more alarming, we imagine weak and token opposition to be insuperable.

Actually, those present at the "summit conference," did not and do not have anything vaguely resembling the power to call off demonstrations. National officers can't tell local chapters how to behave on matters so central to their operations. Shortly after the moratorium announcement several NAACP chapters announced their refusal to go along. At that time demonstrations at the Democratic National Convention in Atlantic City were planned in support of the Mississippi Freedom Democratic Party, and nothing could have stopped them. A major desegregation fight was raging in St. Augustine, Florida; did anyone suppose that it would now proceed without benefit of mass marches, picketing, and demonstrations? And what of the hundreds of local demonstrations related to ongoing campaigns?

We could not sabotage these activities. If we could use demonstrations after the election, we saw no reason not to use them during the election. Negro demonstrations, as I have said, provide the setting for current politics; we aim to maintain that setting. Finally, freedom is not a prize bestowed on the head of the class, a gift for good behavior. Freedom is earned and learned in struggle, and the demonstration remains an indispensable technique of struggle. Which is something those who raise the next question we shall consider should ponder.

IV. HAVE WE NOT MOVED NOW TO A STAGE "BEYOND DEMONSTRATIONS"? *

Yes and no. Clearly the rights movement today faces new problems demanding new techniques. Demonstrations are useful in abetting legal suits to obtain legal rights; as an indispensable form of self-expression for the masses, and useful too in challenging segregation in public accommodations or education, or discrimination in hiring or housing. A restaurant owner, a board of education, a bank president, a real estate man—all may be successfully converted or coerced. But while these problems will remain for years to come and the civil rights movement will need to deal with them continually, it is now clear that other enemies of the Negro are those *impersonal* forces of modern economic life which produce mass unemployment, urban squalor, education inadequate to the demands of our technological economy. If segregation and discrimination were eliminated tomorrow, many, many Negroes would still be ill-equipped to do the work demanded of today's worker. For these problems, traditional demonstrations are not as effective. We will need the financial resources and the concentrated effort of all levels of government, and it will take more money and concentrated effort than is now dreamed of in the philosophies of the anti-poverty program.† And to persuade the government to undertake needed measures, we will need to engage in forms of political activity other than direct action. But demonstrations will be an indispensable adjunct to almost every new effort.

* The quotation is from Bayard Rustin.
† There will also need to be programs in self-help and self-development in the Negro community. See CORE's program in Chapter 7.

Demonstrations *alone* did not achieve the civil rights bill either. Without a half century of legal preparation and lobbying by the NAACP and others, the Congress and the President would not have known where to begin in formulating and passing a civil rights law. We have never denied the necessity for expertise and politics-as-usual at one level of the movement's activities. But without a decade's demonstration of deep and legitimate grievances, the law today would still be a dream.

Bayard Rustin speaks of the inability of demonstrations to achieve "basic reforms" in the system. Demonstrations, he says, deal well with "superficial problems." * I don't know what basic reforms he speaks of and I'm not sure he does, but I do know that without a decade of demonstrations there would be no anti-poverty program today. Who but the civil rights movers dramatized the plight of the poor and created the climate of urgency within which poverty is discussed? We might not have intended it exactly, but by being for ourselves, we helped a lot of poor whites who otherwise would have gone unnoticed.

In his important book *The Other America*, Michael Harrington argues that the poor of America are almost invisible. Concentrated in enclaves off the main highways of American life and concern, the poor are not even visible enough to shake the prevalent and absurd conviction that this is an "affluent society." Manifestly, the task seems to be not simply to imagine and demand programs for the poor and rally our allies, but to convince the nation over and again that the poor truly exist and that their need is urgent.

* Like Rustin, I learned first about direct action from Gandhi. Gandhi would not agree that mass demonstrations are useless in achieving basic reforms, for he worked a revolution with this technique. As Gandhi challenged the salt tax and an empire, so will we use demonstrations to achieve our legislation and alter a realm.

For this, demonstrations are indispensable, albeit in conjunction with other efforts.

And it must be added, of course, that while segregation and discrimination may not be the deepest cause of the Negro's plight, they remain, on the surface where we live and think, prevalent and virulent. The struggle for Civil Rights has not ended. A constant vigil is imperative, a vigil, I might add, which must now be directed to the ever broadening activities of the government, for the poverty program will be administered not by fair-minded intellectuals but by officials and agents, many of whom are conditioned to discriminate by custom and habit. Since the effectiveness of direct action at this "superficial" level is acknowledged, it seems clear that demonstrations will be useful for some time to come.

V. . . . BUT WHEN WILL THE DEMONSTRATIONS END?

I remember the comment of a red-necked young man from St. Augustine, Florida, the leader of a gang of whites who had attacked Negroes trying to swim in the Atlantic Ocean: "If I thought the niggers would be satisfied with just swimming, I'd let them in. But they won't be. First it's this, and then they'll want more, and before you know it they'll be laying hands on our women. We've got to take a stand now, because the more we let them have, the harder it'll be to draw the line."

Sometimes, I think that the racists have a deeper insight into things than the moderates. The gentleman is right. Nothing short of full equality will stop us. One cannot simply draw up a list of ten or twenty things whose fulfillment would spell equality. In countless details we are unequal and elements in our society discover new ways each moment to keep us unequal. The moderate sincerely searches for the concession which will finally satisfy and silence us. He is willing to negotiate and temporarily sacrifice his security to get rid of the problem. The racist knows better how deep the problem is and how long he will need to resist our efforts. But we shall persist, that I promise.

3

WE ARE SOLDIERS

Negroes sweet and gentle,
Meek, humble and kind,
Beware the day
They change their minds!

Wind
In the cotton fields,
Gentle breeze:
Beware the hour
It uproots trees!

—LANGSTON HUGHES

CORE came into being
in 1942. Like most war babies, I suppose, it was born into
a time of violence, but out of a hope for peace. Its
founders were young men and women deeply concerned
with social justice, most of whom were also pacifists. To
the profound and terrible violence of the war, we and many
others of similar convictions had experienced correspond-
ingly deep and troubled reactions. Total war was being
waged in the name of freedom and democracy. We were
all mobilized to fight for the American Way of Life. Yet
in the glare of the conflagration overseas we could see
clearly how much unfreedom and inequality went into that
way of life. Many victims of the Depression were still hungry and terrified; labor all over the country was bound to
long hours and low wages. And always there was the Negro, a full-fledged soldier on the battlefields of France, but
at home still the son of Ham, a servant of servants unto his
brethren.

We wanted desperately to render him equal and free. In our search for a method, we were drawn inevitably to Gandhi. I had presented a long memorandum, "Provisional Plans for Brotherhood Mobilization," to the pacifist Fellowship of Reconciliation (FOR), for which I was then working as race relations secretary. It proposed the establishment of an interracial organization which would apply Gandhian techniques of non-violent direct action to attack segregation in this country: ". . . not to make housing in ghettos more tolerable, but to destroy residential segregation; not to make racial discrimination more bearable, but to wipe it out; . . . effectively to repudiate every form of racism . . . [and to] forge the instrumentalities through which that nation-wide repudiation can be effected!" The small interracial group of Chicago students who were to form the nucleus of CORE had independently evolved a similar idea. While I was drafting a memo, they had already begun formulating action projects. So that when I was authorized by the FOR to set up a pilot project in Chicago, we had only to stretch out our hands to one another, and a movement was created.

There was something extremely audacious in our attempt to apply Gandhi's theories to the American race problem. The Hindu mind, radically different from the American, is much more inclined to perceive battles as spiritual. The Hindu religion conditions its adherents both to the self-discipline and to the setting-the-self-at-naught so necessary to the success of direct action. Furthermore, although the Indians had little political power, they were a vast numerical majority in their country and were working toward the single goal of independence from England, a goal which, however difficult to achieve, was quite simple to define and recognize and which could, indeed, be consummated by a stroke of the pen. Above all, their movement had as its soul the kind of divinely inspired leader who comes perhaps once in a millennium. Gandhi was a man who possessed strategic brilliance and great political shrewdness combined with the charisma of a saint.

Yet it is also true that an American classic, Thoreau's *Civil Disobedience*, exercised a great influence on Gandhi. The belief that each man's actions should have a direct bearing upon his own destiny is quite in accord with the American tradition. And Americans generally prefer to act rather than to withdraw; for that reason, Gandhian militance was much more likely to appeal to Americans than was the passive resistance generally being advocated by our native pacifists. Gandhi's disciple Krishnalal Shridharani, whose *War Without Violence* became our rule book and Bible, remarked that "most American pacifists were less interested than militant liberals in my work. This was as it should have been, as Gandhi's *satyagraha* has more in common with war than with pacifism."

In point of fact, most of us were American pacifists, accustomed to understanding non-violence largely in Tolstoyan terms of non-resistance: the Christian injunction to love thine enemy and turn the other cheek; and non-co-operation: the peaceful refusal to obey unjust laws. But we were also militant pacifists, anxious to change the world, or at least our corner of it. Gandhi, whose assumptions about the power of love and righteousness resembled those of Jesus in the Sermon on the Mount, had nevertheless superimposed upon them a specific and viable program of action. This was what appealed to us, and we adopted it, at least in the beginning, to the letter.

In any attempt at reform the first step always was investigation—seeking out and ascertaining all the relevant facts. Then came negotiation. Every effort was to be made to negotiate with the opposition, in good faith and with good will, and to keep the avenues of negotiation open, even after the project had passed into another phase. When all attempts at negotiation appeared to have failed, then the public was to be informed of the situation through all available media, so that they might add their voices to the protest. If public agitation also failed to open the opponent's mind, the leaders of the movement were to issue an ultimatum, listing once again the particular demands of the movement or project and warning of some sort of direct action if these demands were not met. As the next step, Gandhi outlined a period of *ahimsa*, or self-purification, as a prelude to direct action. For the Indians this involved praying and fasting; in our case it was more likely to entail a rehearsal of the discipline of non-violence and non-retaliation. Finally came direct action, which could range from a relatively simple picket line or protest march, through such various degrees of economic or political coercion as sit-ins, mass boycotts, or filling the jails, to the extreme measures, projected in Gandhi's situation, of mass disobedience of state laws or mass resignation from public office in order totally to disable the government which he understood to be wrongfully in power.

Gandhi coined the word *satyagraha* to describe his movement, partly to shake off the misleading connotations of "passive resistance," and partly to give his All-India movement an all-Indian name. Ironically, there is no English phrase which can adequately translate *satyagraha*. It means something like "soul force" or "the firmness engendered by truth, or love." Westernized Indians have offered the word *Kristograha* to express an equivalent meaning in Christian terms. However it is translated, several different English expressions would be required to cover all its implications. It is *satyagraha* as "the truth which cannot be denied" that stands behind Gandhi's insistence on negotiation and public education. We too, in the early years of CORE, believed that truth alone, the transparent justice of our demands, would convert the segregationists, once they agreed to listen. That was why *satyagraha* as "the firmness engendered by love" was so essential to our discipline. Our own unshakable good will, which left no room in us for violence and helped us endure the violence of others, was the key with which we intended to unlock their hearts.

We were very young and idealistic. We had not yet discovered that Southern sheriffs could respond to non-violent protest with police dogs and cattle prods. We revered Gandhi for his saintliness, but we remembered less vividly that at various times his Congress Party had resorted to hunger strikes, jail-ins, a boycott of foreign cloth, a nation-wide general strike, and even the illegal distillation of salt from the sea in order to circumvent and render unenforceable a compulsory salt tax. That kind of heavy artillery lay beyond the range of our expectations. What could we know about mass desperation, working as we did in small groups, in Northern cities, desegregating one restaurant or one movie house at a time?

The infinite number of tactics that can be improvised in non-violent warfare had not yet excited our attention. We were attracted by other possibilities, somewhat more utopian in nature. Gandhi's program to revitalize rural handicraft in order to make Indian villages economically self-sufficient suggested to us an analogous program for America. Rural Negroes carve quite amazing objects out of gourds and wood, and the women sew and knit beautifully. These skills, which have been passed down from generation to generation, are among the few possessions of some of the poorest people in the country. Why not turn them to profit? Why not, in fact, form an economic base

for our movement by establishing a network of co-operatives—housing co-operatives, producers' and farmers' co-
operatives—extending throughout the country, North and
South? So we asked ourselves, ready to remake the country before we had really begun to find out what it was made
of.

Actually, in the very beginning, we did set up a co-
operative house, although in this case economy was only a
secondary motive. Our first project as a group, plunging
eagerly into action before we had formulated a proper organization or even decided upon a name for ourselves, was
to test discrimination in housing. Chicago at that time
had a blanket of restrictive covenants which kept the
ever-growing Negro population out of 80 per cent of the
city. In defiance of the covenant we established a men's interracial co-operative house in a residential area restricted
to whites. When the real estate company discovered that
Negroes were living in the house, they began legal proceedings to get us evicted. Evidently not daring to test
the legality of the covenant, they claimed instead that
the neighbors objected to our presence. We went to call on
the neighbors. They were not enthusiastic about having
Negroes in the building, but they had no complaints about
our behavior and they saw the justice of our position.
They refused to testify for the prosecution. We won by
their default a victory for decency, and the co-operative
house flourished for many years. For all I know, it is there
still.

At the same time, we set about investigating a roller-
skating rink which had apparently been excluding Negroes. We sent in several groups at carefully timed inter-
vals. All the white people were promptly admitted; all the
Negroes were refused tickets on the grounds that a pri-

vate party was in progress. When the Negroes in the group pointed out their white friends skating inside and suggested to the manager that she publicly order all uninvited guests to leave the rink and refund their money, she refused to talk with us any longer. At this point we were in something of a quandary. It was our first action project and we did not really know how to proceed. What we finally did was to take the case to court, in the style of the NAACP, where (after a series of postponements caused by the "illness" of the manager—who could be seen working at the rink every evening) we eventually lost. The experience was worth-while for us, though, for it gave us a little publicity and enhanced our sense of ourselves as a working group. Six months later, with the help of some CIO unions, we threw a picket line around the rink that forced the owners to negotiate. Shortly afterward, their policy of discrimination ceased entirely.

During these weeks we were in a ferment of excitement. Whenever we could steal the time from our other commitments, we met to hammer out our organization in the white heat of endless passionate discussion. Non-violence was more than a method to us, it was a total way of life, filling us with love and flooding the world with the golden light of unlimited possibility. We decided upon the name CORE, not only because it expressed our determination to get at the root of racial discrimination, but because it reflected our vague yet glorious sense of having penetrated to the heart of things. Then, of course, having found the perfect symbolic abbreviation, we had to find an appropriate meaning for the letters. (Remember, this was the period of the wartime "alphabet agencies," when organizations were better known by their initials than by their actual titles. We have a similar phenomenon today in the current proliferation of initialed civil rights organizations.) We had some difficulty deciding upon the second word in our name. Significantly, "of" won out over "on": we wanted to make it clear that our organization embodied the racial equality which was its goal for the larger society. By the end of the spring of 1942 the first Committee of Racial Equality was a reality.

One evening around this time James R. Robinson, one of the founders of CORE (later its executive secretary), and I, deep in a discussion of CORE, stopped for coffee at a little corner shop called the Jack Sprat, in a middle-class section near the university. The manager of the place served us with the greatest reluctance and then only after we reminded him that he would be violating state law if he refused. Even so, he tried at first to charge me twenty-five cents for a five-cent doughnut. A few days later our fledgling CORE chapter sent in a small interracial group. The manager had us served, but as we left he raked our money off the counter and threw it after us into the street, screaming, "Take your money and get out!"

At the meeting called to formulate a plan of action we turned down a proposal to parade through the Negro section with signs reading JACK SPRAT SERVES NEGROES FREE OF CHARGE, and, still being neophytes, mentally reviewed Shridharani to discover what our procedure ought to be. We had the facts. The next step: negotiation. Accordingly, we tried to telephone the manager, who hung up on us twice. Then we wrote him a letter, explaining our position and asking for a conference. When he did not reply, we wrote a second letter, which also was not answered. Then we sent four people into the restaurant to try to negotiate on the spot. A different manager was in charge this time; he too refused to talk with us. A few nights later we sent in another group. This time there was a third person in charge, a woman, who was somewhat more civil and who explained that they refused service to Negroes only because they feared the loss of white patrons. The CORE group, expressing considerably more sympathy with her point of view than a similar group would today, suggested several ways of proving to her that her fears were groundless, but she refused to try any of them.

We wrote the management one more letter, the "ultimatum" of Gandhi's outline, saying that if we did not hear from them after seven days, we would regretfully be compelled to go into other forms of action. On the eighth day we staged what I believe to have been the first civil rights sit-in. About twenty-five people, all pledged to the discipline of non-violence, entered the restaurant at dinnertime and quietly seated themselves at the counter and in the booths. Several of the white people were served without question; the Negroes were told that they would be served only in the basement. After a few minutes the manager realized that none of the white people had touched their food. They explained that they did not think it polite to eat until their friends had been served. Growing angry, the manager declared that she would not serve us if we sat there until midnight. Meanwhile, a number of the restaurant's regular patrons had come in, waited for a little while, and then, finding that no seats were becoming available, had walked out. Several other customers who had been served before we entered lingered over their dinners, curious to see the outcome of this novel performance. A girl at the counter near me caught on to the situation almost immediately, pushed aside her half-eaten dinner, and spontaneously joined the demonstration.

The manager, increasingly upset, announced that if the Negroes did not want to eat in the basement, she would seat them at the two rear booths, where they would be hidden from view, and have them served very nicely. We declined. Then she called the police, hoping to have us thrown out on a charge of disorderly conduct, but the two policemen who came in found no sign of disorder at all. In accordance with Gandhi's program, we had telephoned the police captain in advance, outlined the procedure we intended to follow, and even read him the state's civil rights law, with which he had apparently been unfamiliar. Consequently, when one of the officers phoned headquarters at the manager's insistence, he was told that nothing in the law allowed them to eject us. The police left. A short time later, the manager had us all served. The test groups sent in during the following weeks were all served promptly and courteously, without incident.

When I look back at that first sit-in, I am amazed at our patience and good faith. We have traveled a great distance since then. No action group today would prolong the attempts at negotiation for more than a month before finally deciding to demonstrate. No militant Negro today would dream of trying to persuade a manager to serve him on the grounds that Negro patronage would not be bad for business. We have grown too proud for that. But in those days we were childishly literal-minded. We believed that people meant exactly what they said to us and heard exactly what we said to them. We regarded the sit-in as the successful culmination of a long campaign to reach the heart of the restaurant owner with the truth. What we took to be his conversion was as important to us as the fact that the restaurant had indeed been desegregated.

As news of our activities spread through the North, we

received letters and inquiries from groups eager to put our methods to work in their own communities. In June of 1943, at a convention of interested groups from nine cities, we formed a national organization. The Congress of Racial Equality, as it was named the following year, consisted of affiliated Committees of Racial Equality and demanded of its chapters only that they formulate simple democratic constitutions and accept the CORE Statement of Purpose and Action Discipline. The stated purpose of CORE was brief: To eliminate all racial segregation and discrimination by means of interracial, non-violent direct action. The action discipline pledged each member to maintain non-violence of word and deed, regardless of provocation; it demanded humility in the face of one's own inadequacy, and understanding and good will before the anger of opponents. It also enforced strict group discipline. All members had to obey the designated project leader. No one could withdraw from a project once he had agreed to participate in it unless he felt incapable of remaining non-violent, in which case he was to withdraw at once. The group, on the other hand, guaranteed each individual an important voice in all project planning and policymaking, and pledged to support him in any difficulty into which CORE activities might lead him.

The same concern for democratic practice which characterized the relations between the individual member and his local chapter controlled the relationship between the local chapter and the national organization. CORE was committed to action, and the national organization wished to function primarily as an enabling instrument for small action groups. New chapters were admitted on the basis of action projects already accomplished and others planned for the immediate future. If, as occasionally happened, a chapter found itself without specific projects, it generally disbanded, for it had lost its only reason for existence.

National CORE did have a few projects of its own. In 1944 it began publishing the *CORElator*, a magazine edited then as now by Jim Peck, although today it has many local editions to supplement the national one. The national organization also sponsored several action projects and a number of summer workshops and training institutes, but for the most part it was concerned with recruiting new chapters. As the organization expanded somewhat in the late forties and early fifties, it constantly strove to sustain internal democracy and to cherish the individual voice. Individual members were urged to come to the national conventions. Regional groups, formed as a liaison between the national organization and widely scattered local groups in certain areas, were careful not to overshadow the local chapters whose representatives constituted their membership. The steering and executive committees were chosen with care, but the national convention remained the source of all major policy.

In the spring of 1947 CORE and the FOR co-sponsored a Journey of Reconciliation, which we now think of as the first Freedom Ride. An interracial group of sixteen people went on a bus-and-train trip through the upper South to test the Supreme Court's decision of the previous year, banning discrimination in interstate travel. The riders were arrested, but the NAACP, which was handling the legal end, eventually dropped the case in favor of another which, in their experienced judgment, they considered legally sounder. Four of the men were convicted and served out a thirty-day sentence on a road gang. Inspired by the Journey, CORE seriously considered making a major effort in the South, not only to create new CORE chapters, but to instigate a large-scale direct-action movement attempting the desegregation of lunch counters, restaurants, and other places of public accommodation. Finally, after much debate, we abandoned the idea. With our limited vision, we could not see any prospect of success. It seemed to us that the time was not right, the people were not ready, and any such move would only arouse a type of opposition which would ultimately destroy the cause of non-violence.

That was CORE before 1956, what might be called ante-bellum CORE. We were small, Northern, middle-class, elitist, idealistic, and predominantly white. We had not yet heard the voice of the masses. Nor, for that matter, had many people heard us. Until 1956 we survived entirely as a volunteer organization to which we were all able to give only part of our time. We had no budget to speak of and no organized publicity. The Fellowship of Reconciliation still contained a number of the kind of pacifists who were embarrassed by any organized aggressiveness, even though non-violent. Our affiliation with the FOR and our own lingering idealism engendered in us the feeling that anything so self-conscious and worldly as a budget, so self-assertive as public relations, was somehow immoral. From the vantage point of today's massive militance, we can see that it was *our* attitude that was immoral. But at that time we had no way of predicting today's Revolution and no one to teach us to think in grander terms.

I I

The Montgomery bus boycott came in 1956, suddenly and with the force of a revelation. It was a spontaneous, mass, non-violent demonstration that neither we nor anyone else had thought likely. It astounded the country. Martin Luther King, who had read Gandhi and was familiar with the techniques of non-violent action, burst upon the scene with something of the Gandhian charisma. The Negroes of Montgomery responded to his call for a boycott with a total commitment and tremendous personal fortitude. The efficiency with which they rearranged their lives and the stoicism with which they endured the attendant physical hardships commanded universal admiration and aroused in thousands of Negro hearts hitherto undreamed-of possibilities for action. The case was ultimately won in the federal courts, but the masses of Negroes who had voluntarily walked to work for a year had carried it there.

Non-violent direct action, which we had been practicing in small, unpublicized groups for fourteen years, became almost overnight a nationally admired phenomenon. The philosophy of love which Dr. King preached and which the Montgomery Negroes appeared to have accepted evoked almost everyone's respect. But angry young Negroes were more impressed with the uses of direct action than with the theory behind it. The boycott had worked. The buses were desegregated. That was what counted.

Montgomery's invitation to mass action went unanswered for three years. Then, in February, 1960, four Negro college students sat-in at a lunch counter in Greensboro, North Carolina. This time the response was almost instantaneous. The students had called on us for assistance. Within a matter of days CORE (which had by then become an independent organization with a budget and a small full-time staff) was hard at work, organizing more sit-ins in the South, mobilizing Northern support, setting up workshops to train demonstrators from both regions in the techniques and discipline of non-violence. It seemed almost as though the previous eighteen years had been a series of private rehearsals for a performance only now beginning upon the stage of history.

Those who found it surprising that so many thousands would submit to the stringent discipline of non-violence had perhaps not realized the delayed impact of World War II on Negroes who, like other Americans, had fought "freedom's" fight against Nazi racism. Having helped to win that battle, Negroes found racism at home more intolerable and less impregnable. Treated as first-class citizens by the people of other countries, they were unwilling to submit to second-class citizenship at home. There was a new generation of college-educated Negro youth, too. The more these young men and women learned about themselves and the world and the American creed, the more determined they grew to achieve full emancipation. And then there was the emergence of Africa, which even the least educated Negro could experience as a source of pride. As proud African black men regained their freedom and began to rebuild their nations, American black men took another look at themselves and liked what they saw.

Tens of thousands of young Negroes who marched, sat-in, or went to jail as the movement spread began to experience the joys of action and the liberating effect of working on behalf of their own destiny. They began to regard themselves differently. The rest of the country also saw the Negroes in a new light. Newspaper and television accounts of the sit-ins suggested a picture which reversed the common stereotypes. Inside, at the lunch counters, sat well-dressed, well-mannered Negro college students with their calculus and philosophy books, quietly asking for a cup of coffee; outside, crowds of white boys with duck-tail haircuts and leather jackets grinned and shuffled their feet and tried to start trouble.

The determination and courage of these Negro students inspired support from thousands of sympathizers, Negro and white, all over the country. CORE helped to organize these people in a less dramatic yet vital activity: boycotting and picketing Woolworth's and the Northern branches of other chain stores which were practicing segregation in the South. The response from unions, churches, student groups, and celebrities was unprecedented. We learned then some of the ways of using national leverage to alter local practices. Segregation is sustained by the interlocking activities of an entire nation. Its workings are not always visible, but we have learned to uncover them and to apply direct pressure in surprising places. For example, without subsidies from both the federal government and Northern capital, segregation could not persist in the South. Bonds for Southern public schools are floated by brokers in New York, New Jersey, Massachusetts, Pennsylvania, Illinois, and California. Northern investors thus supply the fuel that feeds Southern segregation. Income from such investments is tax-exempt. Therefore, despite the 1954 Supreme Court decision, the federal government is indirectly subsidizing school segregation.

The sit-ins taught us much about the nature of the revolution. The mass movement of which we had hardly dared to dream in our days of youthful idealism was now becoming a reality. If CORE was to continue in a position of significance and authority, we would have to learn to embrace these masses of willing revolutionaries. No longer could we indulge in the luxury of the perfectly designed, perfectly executed action project, in which each individual had a voice in every step of the planning and all the dem-

onstrators were steeped in the philosophy and tactics and
discipline of non-violence. Nor would the local chapters be
able to retain quite the same autonomy. With the movement
achieving national dimensions, CORE too would have to
operate on a national scale, formulating policies and organizing projects far beyond the scope of individual chapters,
making on-the-spot decisions that would allow no time
for referendums. The challenging task confronting CORE
and all the other civil rights organizations was that of giving a certain amount of direction to the movement and
imposing upon it the control of non-violence, without in-
hibiting the spontaneity or self-expression of thousands
of newly aroused Negroes.

The following year we collided head-on with the realities we had glimpsed during the sit-ins; 1961 was the year
of the historic Freedom Rides which catapulted CORE to
fame. Our initial demonstration involved a small interracial group which was to ride two buses through Virginia,
the Carolinas, Georgia, Alabama, Mississippi, and Louisiana, testing the Supreme Court decision banning segregation in bus terminals serving interstate passengers. Our
intention was to provoke the Southern authorities into arresting us and thereby prod the Justice Department into
enforcing the law of the land. We started the Freedom
Rides with thirteen people. At best we had expected to conclude it with thirteen people. But after one bus was burned
in Anniston, Alabama, and the riders on another were
beaten and abused, we were deluged with letters and tele-
grams from people all over the country, volunteering their
bodies for the Freedom Rides. Hundreds of innocent, in-
experienced people poured in, many of whom had never
before been active in civil rights. If we had refused these
people, they would have come anyway. The best we could
do under the circumstances was to funnel them through

checkpoints in Chicago and New Orleans, desperately trying to keep track of everyone, and put them through an
intensive one- or two-day training session in the methods
of non-violence. The sheer weight of all these numbers
shifted our original emphasis and made of the Freedom
Rides a different and far grander thing than we had intended them to be. Instead of seeking token arrests to spur
legal and administrative action, we began to fill the jails of
Mississippi—a Gandhian tactic aimed at making segregationist practices so expensive and inconvenient as to become
unfeasible.

This tactic was excellent, but the mistakes we made in
the course of implementing it almost put us out of business. No real effort had been made to mobilize the Negro
populace in towns along the route, although their marvel-
ous response to the Freedom Riders made it clear that
we could easily have done so. We filled the jails only with
people who traveled great distances to be arrested. Further, only a handful of the Riders who were arrested
served their full sentences. Everyone else had to come
out on bond.

And this created a staggering financial problem. The
usual sources of bail money—bonding companies within
the state—were closed to us because of discriminatory policies or official pressure. We tried to raise bond money
from a Hartford, Connecticut, insurance company which
had branches in Mississippi. The company agreed by telephone but retracted its promise the next morning, after a
Mississippi representative had warned that such a loan to
the Freedom Riders would ruin their local business. Other
large bonding companies refused us on similar grounds.

Then the State of Mississippi compounded our troubles.
The usual practice in cases of mass arrest is to require for
arraignment only one person representing each type of ar-

rest: in this instance, someone arrested in the bus terminal, someone from the airport, and someone from the railroad station. We had arrived at a verbal understanding to this effect with the Mississippi authorities. Our lawyers would then plead for the rest of us who would not be required to return. But ten days before the arraignment date the State of Mississippi, in an all-out drive to force us into bankruptcy, insisted that every one of the Riders out on bail would either have to appear before the court or forfeit the $500 bond which CORE had put up for each. The Riders, of course, had scattered all over the country in the intervening six months. Eventually we rounded most of them up (although we never did locate one fellow reported to be in Istanbul), but we incurred enormous expense in the process. We had to transport them to Jackson and back, pay for their keep while they were there, meet the ever increasing legal costs which had initially been very high, and then, to top it all off, come up with an additional $325,000 in bail money, since Mississippi, matching our creative tactics with an ingenuity of its own, had tripled the bond requirements. Somehow we managed to find the money, partly through the great generosity of Thurgood Marshall, and Jack Greenberg, whose NAACP Legal Defense and Education Fund made its special bail bond fund available to us for as long as it lasted and in addition agreed to pay the court costs, all the way up to the Supreme Court.

For the most part, the Freedom Rides were enormously successful. Attorney General Robert Kennedy, who had urgently advised the first group to discontinue the rides at Montgomery, requested from the Interstate Commerce Commission an order banning segregation in seating on interstate buses and outlawing racial discrimination in bus terminal facilities used by interstate passengers. This order went into effect on November 1, 1961, and the CORE teams which began testing it on November 2 found widespread compliance to be the rule.

The jail-in took its place in the armory of viable nonviolent techniques, to be used to great effect in subsequent demonstrations. We never did manage to fill the jails completely; I think that Southern cities and states have almost unlimited jail facilities, and if they don't, they can quickly improvise more. But we did succeed in costing the city of Jackson over a million dollars. They were forced to hire new policemen and pay others overtime, pay for our upkeep in the city jail, rent space in the state penitentiary and pay the state for our food there. The expense was so great that the city had to cancel plans to repeal a nuisance tax which had been irritating its citizens for some time. And of course the State of Mississippi, in addition to the drain on jails and state troopers, incurred considerable legal costs.

The familiar Southern complaint that the Southern Negroes would be perfectly content were they not being stirred up by "outside agitators" from the North, was exposed in all its absurdity and immorality. Segregation is not a Southern problem but a national one; where one lives in America sets no bounds on his moral responsibility toward his fellow Americans. As Frank Randall, a professor of history at Columbia, said of his Freedom Ride: ". . . under whatsoever circumstances we may be asked, 'What did you do for the liberation of your fellow man?' we can all answer, 'In June, 1961, we took a bus ride to Florida.' " And all those Freedom Riders, who came with very little knowledge of what was in store for them, went back to their homes with a deep and abiding commitment to the movement of the sort that only direct participation can inspire.

Most crucially, perhaps, the rides helped clarify the role of creative conflict and tension in non-violent struggle. We learned through brute experience what every student of social change knows as a matter of principle: that no such entrenched order as our national system of segregation ever gives way without conflict. If there is no tension, that is simply a sign that the disinherited are not protesting. To put it in the religious terms of Gregory Vlastos: "He who preaches love in a society based upon injustice can purchase immunity from conflict only at the price of hypocrisy." Or consider the words of ex-slave Frederick Douglass:

> Those who profess to favor freedom and yet deprecate agitation, are men who want crops without plowing up the ground. They want rain without thunder and lightning. They want the ocean without the awful roar of its many waters. The struggle may be a moral one; or it may be a physical one; or it may be both moral and physical. But it must be a struggle. Power concedes nothing without demand. It never did and it never will.

The hundreds of people who rode Freedom buses into the South and the thousands who cheered them on created a thunder-and-lightning storm which even we professional rain-makers had not intended. The same kind of turbulence broke out in Albany, Georgia, the following year, and in Birmingham the year after that, and then in a score of Birminghams all over the country. We learned from the triumphs of the Freedom Rides to channel that turbulence into massive demonstrations and jail-ins, involving thousands, not hundreds, of Negroes. We learned also from the mistakes of the Freedom Rides to use local citizens in our demonstrations and to mobilize the local Negro communities.

. . .

The Freedom Highways campaign of 1962 climaxed our efforts in the realm of public accommodations. Our groups traveling across the country to desegregate highway restaurants and motels concentrated particularly on the Howard Johnson and Holiday Inn chains. Friends of the movement stayed away from their local Howard Johnson restaurants in the same kind of sympathetic boycott which two years earlier had backed up the student sit-ins at Woolworth's. By the end of 1962 a Negro could drive along the national highways and know that when he was hungry or tired, there would be a place where he would be welcome to stop and rest.

During the past several years CORE has grown dramatically. We have increased our membership and our budget every year since 1959. Today we include eighty thousand members, including a special class of associate members whose contribution to CORE is purely financial and who therefore do not have a voice in policy making. Our staff has jumped in five years from 7 to 137. We have 140 full-fledged chapters and 80 others in various stages of affiliation.

Largely as a result of this massive increase in our membership CORE has shifted its emphasis somewhat, focusing less on desegregation and more on political action, economic discrimination, and problems within the Negro communities. In the South, of course, voter registration has been the big issue. Year-round efforts on the part of CORE staff members, bolstered by waves of volunteers during the summers of 1963, 1964 and 1965, have yielded impressive results. In South Carolina fifty-six thousand Negroes have been entered in the books since 1963, in the face of flagrant delaying tactics by the registrars, and despite the fact that for most of the year the registration books were open only one day a month. In early 1965 CORE, in co-operation with local leaders, succeeded in persuading the mayor of Bogalusa, Louisiana, to promise to repeal local segregation ordinances, to hire some Negroes on the police force, to desegregate public parks and other facilities, and to improve the condition of street pavements and sanitation in the Negro quarter. This was an unprecedented concession by an elected official in the Deep South. But unfortunately, Mayor Cutrer quickly backed down on his promise. Despite this betrayal the Negro citizens of Bogalusa continue, and will continue, to press their demands. In Mississippi, Louisiana, and northern Florida, CORE people have developed community centers which incorporate voter-registration offices and supplement them with educational and recreational facilities. One such community center is going up in Philadelphia, Mississippi, to honor the memory of the three martyred workers, James Chaney, Andrew Goodman, and Michael Schwerner, who were brutally murdered at the onset of the Mississippi Freedom Summer of 1964. Chaney and Schwerner were on the CORE staff.

In the big northern cities the Negro's problems are at once more ambiguous and more complex. A major one is economic: CORE is determined to see to it that Negroes are no longer the last hired, first fired. We insist that the unions put an end to their discriminatory policies and that industrial and other employers extend without limit the kinds of jobs open to Negroes. Pickets, marches, and many kinds of demonstrations have put our point across.

But most important, we are working inside the populous Northern ghettos to encourage a feeling of community solidarity, to give apathetic or skeptical Negroes the confidence and incentive to take their lives into their own hands. We have made door-to-door canvasses in some cities to determine which problems are most pressing, and

have mobilized the people to demonstrate on their own behalf. Local chapters have sprouted and created direct-
action techniques to suit their own needs: rent-strikes to
protest substandard housing; demonstrations before mayors
and building commissioners to call attention to violations
of the housing code; demonstrations to obtain needed play
streets and traffic lights; and even the famous garbage-
dump on New York's Triborough Bridge to dramatize
the unsanitary conditions of Harlem schools. The demonstrations have been successful, for the most part, and the
demonstrators have got their reforms. But what matters
more is the sense of possibility which has bloomed in the
ghetto. CORE, at this juncture in our history, has discovered a new resonance in its name. We are turning inward
to the core of the Negro community, where ultimately the
strength of our people must lie.

I I I

The Negro Revolution is now ten years old. The New
Jacobins, the angry young men and women who rose up
to claim what belonged to them, were responsible for trans-
forming a well-intentioned but slow-moving Cause into a
full-fledged revolutionary Movement. What the New Jacobins demand today is total war to achieve total rights. If
there is any word more hated in the struggle than "moderation," it is "tokenism." This revolution exacts from its revolutionists and requires of its friends and allies a staunch and
thoroughgoing commitment in both motivation and concrete actions. Nothing short of that is acceptable any more.
If anyone who fancies himself a supporter or an ally or
even a leader does not, in the opinion of the revolutionists,
"feel" the movement, does not, in the vernacular, "dig"
the struggle in the streets, no number of words or even

good deeds will fully qualify him for the Jacobins' trust. If, on the other hand, he appears to "dig" the movement, but falters before the totality of its demands, then to the people in the streets he is at best friction within the revolution's machinery, at worst a traitor.

The apparent sudden emergence of the Negro's revolutionary mood caught many of his friends, particularly among labor and the liberals, unaware. Satisfied with their own good intentions, they were geared to a gradual approach to equality. Now they are puzzled and offended by the criticisms which impatient Negroes have leveled at them. The tension between the Jacobins and these men of good (if incomplete) will may yet lead to tragedy within the movement.

But if the New Jacobins judge their friends harshly, they are even more rigorous in their demands upon themselves and each other. Discomfort, danger, suffering, are commonplace. To face brutality is routine; to risk death, prosaic. All the revolutionists, being human, experience fear to some extent, but to yield to human frailty under stress is the supreme disgrace. These exacting standards are not new in human experience. But they are new in the Negro's struggle for equality in America.

What happened to the movement and to CORE after Montgomery was a kind of wedding of two forces, both bred by the war: the means-oriented idealists of pacifistic turn of mind, for whom non-violence was a total philosophy, a way of life—we had founded CORE; and the ends-oriented militants, the New Jacobins, disillusioned with America's rhetoric of equality, who saw in direct action a useful weapon and viewed non-violence only as a tactic.

Without such a fusion, no revolutionary mass movement could have emerged. Without the Young Turks the movement could never have grown to mass proportions, and without the idealists it could not have developed revolutionary dimensions. The anger of one without the disciplined idealism of the other could have produced only nihilism. Without the indigenous anger of the Negro masses, the idealists for all their zeal would have remained largely irrelevant and would have gone on talking to themselves and whispering through an occasional keyhole to another human heart.

As in any working marriage, each party speaks much truth to the other. The idealists warn that the ends do not justify the means, and the militants assert with equal validity that means are worthless which do not achieve substantial reform. Each tempers the other, and out of the creative tension between the two has come a third position which I believe more accurately reflects the movement. Today, non-violence is neither a mere tactic which may be dropped on any occasion nor an inviolable spiritual commitment. It is somewhere between the two—not a philosophy, not a tactic, but a strategy involving both philosophical and tactical elements, in a massive and widening direct-action campaign to redeem the American promise of full freedom for the Negro.

This does not mean that all of the hundreds of thousands of Negroes involved in the street campaigns for equality accept non-violence as strategy or tactic or anything else. It is only the leaders, members, and close associates of the non-violent movement who accept it in any way as an integral part of the struggle. The masses who now join picket lines and sit-ins and protest marches share only a new-found willingness to become individually physically involved and to risk suffering or jail for common goals. They come from the pool halls and taverns as well as churches, from the ranks of the unemployed and the alienated and the rootless. They are not yet wedded to non-violence: they are wedded, indeed, only to their own fierce indignation. Yet they are necessary to the revolution; their absence would brand the movement as counterfeit and ultimately destroy it. Obviously it will be difficult to maintain non-violence through the stresses of a mass direct-action movement. And that, precisely, is one of the chief tactical dilemmas before the Freedom Movement.

Small disciplined groups are easy to control. Untrained masses are more difficult. Violence used against us by our opponents is a problem only insofar as it may provoke counter-violence from our ranks. Thus far, as we have seen, sporadic incidents of violence, where they have occurred in the movement, have been contained and have not become a contagion. We have been lucky, but we cannot afford any longer to leave such a vital matter to chance. Widespread violence by the freedom fighters would sever from the struggle all but a few of our allies. It would also provoke and, to many, justify such repressive measures as would injure the movement. More than that, many of our own non-violent activists would turn away in disenchantment. None would profit from such developments except the defenders of segregation and perhaps the more bellicose of the black nationalist groups.

I have often heard it said in criticism of CORE that in becoming a mass movement, it fatally compromised its principles. A cadre of lovers became an army of haters, it is alleged. First, let me insist that we do not hate; far from it. We are not the paragons of love we once were, to be sure, but we do not hate. There are haters afoot and I shall be speaking of them later, but we are not they. Second, I wish to emphasize that we have not experienced the changes which have taken place in CORE as a compromise or even, as is otherwise alleged, as revolutionary necessity. We have changed but only because we have learned from the

experience of over twenty years that the world is more
complex than we had imagined and the techniques and
motives necessary to change it more varied and larger in
scope than we had ever dreamed. The original CORE vision was excessively interpersonal and private. There was
not men nor time nor spirit enough to change each lunch-
counter-owner's heart, one by one. As we learned when we
finally met them, our people did not wish to wait that long,
and *out of love for them* we did not wish them to. We
learned too that before the millennium we could at least
alter behavior *and conditions* which created injustice. We
dreamed of a better America and still we dream. To
desist from working for that dream out of loyalty to an
idea of CORE which in some ways was proven ineffectual
would be the real compromise. We have learned from the
Jacobins. Today we are all Jacobins.

One CORE principle has remained unaltered from the
first. We believed and we believe that men must achieve
freedom for themselves. Do it for them and you extin-
guish the spark which makes freedom possible and glorious.
Men must act on their own behalf; they must aim to move
the world and sense its movement under their impact. They
must speak as well as act and they must speak with their
own voice. Is it hoarse sometimes with frustration and anger? That is our voice. Very well. We must love ourselves
first.

The masses of Negroes who are now involved in the
movement have achieved a measure of spiritual emancipation with which Lincoln's Proclamation could not possibly
have endowed them. The segregation barriers erected in
America have, for them, ceased to be an extension of their
minds. They are no longer chained to the ancient stereotypes. They do not feel inferior and do not believe that

they are; they are no longer comfortable in the confines of the caste. We feel dignified. We are dignified.

This new dignity has many manifestations, not the least significant of which is a great and burgeoning sense of individual worth, released, ironically, through a mass movement. In a way it is a rediscovery of the individual in American society. The average American, or for that matter the average man in any industrial society, feels submerged, powerless, a cog in a giant machine. But in his revolution the individual Negro has found a new meaning for himself. People formerly little and insignificant now, in their own eyes, stand ten feet tall. As one student in Atlanta put it: "I, myself, desegregated that lunch counter on Peachtree Street. Nobody else. I did it by sitting-in, by walking the picket line, by marching. I didn't have to wait for any big shots to do it for me. I did it myself." Never again will that youth and the many like him see themselves as unimportant.

Here then is the tradition and impetus CORE brings to the future: We are, as ever, an organization pledged to make freedom and equality a possibility through that inner emancipation which comes of direct effort. We know as clearly as ever that freedom cannot be won solely by engineers, although a considerable amount of engineering will be necessary. We stand for action, and in an America which out of comfort or ennui despairs of the possibility of an effective and morally integrated gesture, we represent almost uniquely the possibility for a free life. We have become a mass movement and know we can only become more of a mass movement. We have an arsenal of techniques in direct action and must restudy their applicability. We stand astride fierce and ambiguous energies, some noble, some not, and will seek to channel them, but we will not renounce them. We hold impatience a virtue and will not be quickly satisfied. We recall our dreams of creative reconciliation and feel we serve them still, in our manner. But love is a luxurious tactic and the realities of militant non-violence permit us few luxuries. We *are* non-violent because non-violence is a weapon tested out and proven effective. Prudence, tactical good sense, and our ideals demand that we remain so.

4

BLACK
NATIONALISTS
AND
WHITE LIBERALS

S E V E R A L years ago a white CORE worker, a pretty girl of about twenty, was mugged in the corridor of her apartment house. She described her assailant in some detail for the police—height, approximate weight, eyes, teeth, clothing—but she omitted one vital point: he was black; she didn't mention that simple fact for fear of indicating prejudice.

This young lady was a true child of the "old" CORE. No organization was so aggressively color-blind, so ideologically committed to the utter irrelevance of race, as we. If only the races could get to know each other—living, working, playing in each other's sight—what purpose would there be to note a man's race? We told uplifting stories to each other and to the world. Like the one about the little boy who came home from school with the news of a wonderful new friend. The mother, becoming suspicious, asked, "Now, is Johnny white or colored?" And the boy replied, "Well, I don't know. I'll have to go back to-

morrow and look and see." We laughed. Oh, how we
laughed. Brothers and Sisters, is this not indeed the way it
will be some day? Our work and fellowship in CORE
during those early years were dominated by these sentiments: members of both races strove to make sure that
color wouldn't count in our daily activities, even as it
wouldn't count in the Great Day that was coming. One of
CORE's first pamphlets was called "Erasing the Color
Line"; some time later it was revised and retitled "Cracking
the Color Line."

One cannot deny the charm and ultimate validity of
these sentiments, yet today they seem to me to be somewhat out of touch with the real lives and the real needs of
the Negro community—and inappropriate, even, to the real
tasks of our movement. We breathed pure sentiments and
ideals, never pausing to sniff the impure air of the every-
day. I have come to understand my own life in this way. I
grew up in the South, living in the sheltered atmosphere of
several Negro colleges. My father was a professor of clas-
sics who lived in his books and seemed to know ancient
tongues and folkways more intimately than those of his
own time and place. It was an *Alice in Wonderland* world,
located at best on the fringes of Negro life. I prepared for
the ministry, and after realizing that it was not my true
calling, worked in pacifist and socialist groups. With friends
I studied Gandhi, Shridharani, Tolstoy, Marx, Thoreau,
Veblen. We thought and talked and dreamed with each
other long into the night. And these activities, too, in their
way, isolated me from my people. For as long as I can remember I have been dedicated to gaining equality for Negroes, but I know now that, in part, I came to this commitment theoretically, with some of the zeal of the theorist.

Today, when the name Negro is sweet to CORE's ears,
we laugh that there was ever a day when it was otherwise.

We have found the cult of color-blindness not only quaintly irrelevant but seriously flawed. For we learned that America couldn't simply *be* color-blind. It would have to *become* color-blind and it would only *become* color-blind when *we* gave up our color. The white man, who presumably has no color, would have to give up only his prejudices. We would have to give up our identities. Thus, we would usher in the Great Day with an act of complete self-denial and self-abasement. We would achieve equality by conceding racism's charge: that our skins were an affliction; that our history is one long humiliation; that we are empty of distinctive traditions and any legitimate source of pride. Indeed we would cease to use the word *we*, for we would concede that there is no "we" which can meaningfully refer to Negroes. And all this we were asked to do, and asked ourselves to do, *at the very moment* when the movement was teaching us to love ourselves, and making the name Negro a name to conjure with.

In the movement for equal rights we discovered a history: Had not the slaves rebelled tirelessly against their lot as we now rebelled? Suddenly, we found heroes and examples from our own past: Gabriel Prosser, Nat Turner, Denmark Vesey, Harriet Tubman, Charles Lenox Redmond, Sojourner Truth, Samuel E. Cornish, Frederick Douglass, W. E. B. Du Bois. We sensed the presence of black men all over the world who were engaged in efforts parallel to our own, calling us brother and asking us to call them brother. In the movement we found an identity. Was that not jealousy we spotted in the eager eyes of white youths who flocked to *our* cause knowing that *our* efforts constituted the most significant activity in all of America; that *we* were making American history, fulfilling America's inner purpose, knowing that America could not be free and equal if *we* did not make a name for ourselves; that far from having no history, no one in America had a history but *us;* that *we were* American history and that for the sake of American ideals *we* had to speak in our rightful, our given, our now legitimate name— Negro?

In the last four years CORE has ceased simply serving Negroes and has become a Negro organization. We have entered the ghetto and begun the arduous task of organizing the black lower classes, for years neglected and even despised by the Establishment. And we have begun to hear reports of strife between nationalists and integrationists in CORE chapters all over the country. This usually means strife between blacks and whites—but not always. The lines are not strictly drawn: some of our white members are rabid black nationalists.*

Early in 1964 I called a meeting of all the chapters in the Bay Area of San Francisco. I had heard of rather serious strife there and when we all had gathered in a hotel room one night I said, "All right, let's let our hair down and level with one another. What's it all about?" One fellow immediately hit the floor, a Negro, and said, "Brother Farmer, we've got to dig being black." And he kept repeating it over and over again, and I knew exactly what he meant. He meant that blackness of the skin had been a deformity and had been accepted as a deformity by Negroes, that it had to cease being that, and had to become a source of pride, and so too did all the culture and memories that went with it.

In subtle ways racial considerations entered the inner politics of our organization. For reasons both real and

---

* When I use the term "nationalist," I do not, for the moment, mean a member of a nationalist organization but rather someone aggressively proud of the black community—someone who sees great value in maintaining the community, someone the sociologists might call ethnocentric. I shall discuss the black nationalist organizations a little later.

symbolic it is important that Negroes be placed in positions of leadership and prominence. It is difficult for some whites to understand how deeply Negroes feel about this. For years the great Negro organizations—NAACP, Urban League—have been strongly influenced by whites who have served as presidents of these organizations, as members of governing boards, or, significantly, as treasurers. Whites provided financial support to these organizations, and the wealthy and charitable men who would handsomely underwrite activities of a Negro organization had not amassed their fortunes by ignoring their investments. Another traditional form of white support for the Negro was in the form of aggressive advice from influential and allied organizations—church groups, civil rights commissions, labor unions, parents and teachers associations. It is not disrespectful to their often sincere and effective efforts to point out that their advice was not always motivated by the immediate interest of the black man. The evil of slavery (and to some degree Negroes are still enslaved) is in the way it permitted white men to *handle* Negroes—their bodies, their actions, their opportunities, their very minds and thoughts. To the depths of their souls Negroes feel handled, dealt with, ordered about, manipulated—by white men. I cannot overemphasize the tenacity and intensity of this feeling among Negroes and I believe any fair-minded person pondering the history of the Negro's enforced posture in a world of white power would concede the justice of the feeling. So, as Negroes began to sense that the civil rights movement was *their* movement, an instrument for *their* self-expression, *their* freedom (in addition to being a vehicle for universal ideals), it became difficult to convince them that once again they must be led by whites.

Naturally, some individual injustice arose from this new

conviction—and for those of us who have worked for years, as brothers, with white men, some of the political positions we have taken were heartbreaking. A few years ago at our national convention, a brilliant and utterly dedicated white man, Alan Gartner, was bidding for the national chairmanship of CORE. He had worked hard and aspired honorably for the position. He was a close friend and a man I admire enormously. Furthermore, he was the choice of the outgoing chairman, Charles Oldham, also white. But I knew that at that stage of our struggle he could not be chairman, and that if he ran, the convention would not only defeat him but might turn from the really able Negroes available to a rabid racist, who would raise the divisive racial issue on the floor. So I gathered our staff together along with Mr. Gartner and told him that if he insisted on running, I would fight him on the floor of the convention. We argued painfully and tearfully for hours. What of CORE's principles of interracialism and color-blindness? Some accused me of being a black nationalist, though the candidate did not. "Why can't he run? Is he competent or isn't he?" "There are other competent men." Well, Mr. Gartner agreed not to run and a floor fight was averted. The new chairman, Floyd McKissick, was elected by acclamation and he has served expertly for some time. As a leader of the organization I rejoiced that CORE had navigated treacherous waters successfully, but I was personally saddened by the cost of our decision. For, no doubt, we had denied this man categorically, because of his color, and this was not at all like us. Yet I defend the compromise.

My relationship with Mr. Gartner remained strained for about a year after the convention incident; but today we have reached an understanding about the incident if not complete agreement. He was, until recently, chairman of

CORE's Boston chapter and in the summer of 1965 he accepted an important position on our national staff. And he remains an outspoken prophet in our midst, warning us, in the words of the freedom song, to keep our eyes on the prize.

I have dwelt a moment on this incident because it is characteristic of many which have occurred in the movement over the last year, and because I think it helps define for me what the position of the white man must be in this Negro movement for civil rights. As I see it, the tension between Negroes and whites in CORE is a necessary and creative tension. Some form of nationalism is necessary, even healthy, though the willfully color-blind refuse to acknowledge this. But the old CORE idealists are correct when they warn that Negro group pride and group assertiveness can deteriorate into the most narrow-minded chauvinism. Of course, integration—color-blindness—is ultimately valid, but we have to come to realize that we must live here and now rather than in eternity. Yet even this comment is not without its complications. I do not define this tension as one between the real and the ideal, with the black nationalists playing the realists and the white integrationists playing the idealists. The doctrinaire color-blind often fail to perceive that it is *ideally* necessary for the black man to be proudly black today. And the black nationalists, for their part, often do not see that it is only realistic to maintain touch with white people, for we cannot live in our dreams nor carve a nation for ourselves in our mind's eye alone. We must dwell in this land of ours— America.

No simple definition will fit us and if we make ourselves over to satisfy any one definition—nationalist or integrationist—we will lose a precious part of ourselves. So, in some ways, I applaud the tension between black and white and invite whites in to embarrass us with our occasional narrowness, asking them only to be tactful and remember who and what it is they serve.

What can explain this new "mood ebony" in CORE? The reasons are many and complex, but I would like to suggest three in particular. (1) I alluded to the ironic fact that each achievement of the civil rights movement aimed at making color irrelevant counted to us as a Negro achievement, earned by Negro effort, and indicative of a long rebel tradition in Negro history. The movement became a movement *of* and *by* Negroes on top of being a movement *for* civil equality, and it became a source of great pride and inspired a renewed search for a black identity. We learned that what was needed was not *invisibility* but a valid and legitimate *visibility*. This new pride, which grew out of the movement, is especially noteworthy in the Negro middle classes which until very recently stood aloof from the struggle. But in civil rights it has often been the middle classes—especially the students—who led the militant way. Then, too, a new generation of Negro writers—James Baldwin, Ossie Davis, John Williams, John Oliver Killens, Louis Lomax—gave our new pride the impetus of their eloquence. (2) The masses of black people we attracted to our banner influenced our mood. The integration-which-would-end-in-assimilation has never been a prime goal of the Negro masses. Historically it has been the small Negro middle class which has stumped for total integration. In the past the men who have prodded the average Negro into active response have always—like the fabled Marcus Garvey—emphasized race and adopted some form of nationalism. In the twenties, a decade when thousands of Negroes were lynched and race riots tore the land, Garvey came here from Jamaica. He recalled for Negroes the slave rebellions of old and the struggles of Zulu and Hottentot warriors against white imperialists, and he spoke of glorious empires in Africa. Millions flocked to his black, red, and green flag, and bought an African dream. Today the black nations in Africa have begun to make Garvey's dream into simple, demonstrable realities. Garveyism remains latent in the Negro ghetto, as our new recruits taught us. (3) The present-day black nationalist groups—the best-known of which is the so-called Black Muslims—and figures like the late Malcolm X have influenced us perceptibly.

Sympathetic whites are often surprised at the solicitude Negroes display for the nationalists, the Muslims in particular. "How can anyone take all that mumbo-jumbo seriously?" they ask. And in righteous tones they quickly dismiss this "racism in reverse," this cult of opportunistic violence, this implausible doctrine of Negro separatism—as juvenile and positively un-American. Many Negroes see the juvenility, of course, but they see more: the black nationalists tell the Negro that he is somebody and that his salvation depends upon the proud acceptance of his own blackness. White civilization, say the nationalists, taught the Negro to hate himself; this was and remains a tactic of white domination, for if the Negro did not hate himself, he would have been a most troublesome servant indeed. Stripped of a sense of history, deprived of his majesty, brain-washed by a white man's religion, without a name or any claim to fame, the Negro was a man without suitable memories and a suitable self-definition. Therefore, as the first order of business, before economic or social reforms, the nationalists say we must mend black souls and replace shame with pride. There are very few Negroes who are not moved by this rudimentary appeal. Many educated Negroes are willing to forgive the exotic myths the Muslims spin to dress up their message.

But the Muslims and others not only recommended
themselves by what we might term their insight into the
black heart but by their simple success as well. They succeeded, as no one else, in eliminating narcotics addiction,
prostitution, juvenile delinquency among their members
and the people they reached. Within the group almost
puritanical standards of sexual and personal morality pre-
vailed—frugality, hard work, character-building were emphasized. The Muslims and other nationalists bade the Negro to help himself by himself, by cleaning up his own
mind and his own streets, by educating himself, by starting
his own businesses, by patronizing and hiring blacks. Much
of this is simply a black variety of the Protestant ethic,
and it appeals to the basic American middle-class values
held by most Negroes. Unfortunately, the Muslims do not
apply these moral scruples to those who leave the sect,
many of whom are dealt with ruthlessly. And there have
been charges of immorality in the upper echelons. Still,
even if these charges were accurate, they would not gain-
say the legitimate achievement of the Muslims in regenerating many down-and-outers in the ghetto.

Malcolm X had a considerable impact on my own thinking. His own tragically brief career exemplified the best
and worst in the Muslim influences. From an uneducated,
narcotics-addicted denizen of the New York underworld,
Malcolm became an articulate and extraordinarily disciplined spokesman for the Muslims. He was a regenerated
man, fascinating and powerful. He spoke with great if un-
tutored lucidity, and he had a following of admirers—
some grudging—far wider than is apparent if one simply
counts Muslim membership. A year before his assassination
on February 21, 1965—the first day of Brotherhood Week
—Malcolm broke with the Muslims to found the Organization of Afro-American Unity, the very name of which in-

dicates his desire to bring all Negroes—separationists and integrationists, Muslims, Christians, and others—under a single nationalist tent.

I met Malcolm shortly before the Freedom Rides, just after I had assumed direction of CORE. We were brought together on the Barry Gray Show, a late-evening discussion program in New York City, and I must say I completely underestimated him. Malcolm was defending the Muslim line of establishing a black nation somewhere in the United States, and it was not difficult to ridicule the impracticality of that idea; but when he spoke to me directly, calling me black man, calmly drawing some of the bitterness out of me, I listened. And later I found my thoughts returning quite often to his message of self-pride and self-love. I got to know Malcolm quite well in the two years before his death. He kept predicting that I would be a nationalist by year's end and I predicted he would become an integrationist, and we may both have been right; for at the time of his death, Malcolm was entering a civil rights movement he had derided as foolish, and I was seeing some of the psychological if not political sense of his words. We never glossed over our differences, but there was mutual respect working and I always felt that Malcolm—who was not one to treat civil rights leaders tenderly—was a little softer on me than on Wilkins or King.

He was a simpler man than is usually supposed. For years he reiterated to skeptics that he believed with perfect faith that Elijah Muhammad was the messenger sent by God Himself—Allah—and I think he did. Quick-witted and serious, he was neither a deep nor a sophisticated thinker. For all his talk of black separatism and for all his apparent racism, I do not think he fully grasped or really wished that these ideas should exclude him from the Negro's future in this country. This seems to me the tragedy of so many nationalists. Hung up on a bogus mythology, committed to their loose threats and big talk, they do not let themselves even contemplate the possibility that the Negro will survive in America with his soul intact and his future legitimate and secure. They feel kinship with the "movement" but are prodded into scoffing and posturing by their own rhetoric or that of their leaders.

After he left the Muslims, Malcolm cast this way and that for a stance. For a while he was strongly influenced by the Trotskyite Socialist Workers Party which today hopes to prod black nationalism into violently revolutionary action. But when he traveled to the Middle East in the fall of 1964, he seemed to be casting about for some way to join the civil rights movement. "I have come to this holy city to worship," he wrote to me from Mecca. "In all my years in the United States, I have never seen the brotherhood of man working as it does here. I've witnessed thousands of pilgrims of all colors." He underlined *all colors*. Malcolm felt quite consciously that his extremism helped militant organizations like CORE by making their non-violence respectable in comparison to his own talk of violence. And he did serve this function. One thing is clear; he could not long stand aside from any fight his people were waging. He loved them, and however much he scoffed at the futility of making do in a white world, he cheered the great efforts we have made to do just that. Shortly before his death Malcolm appeared in Selma, Alabama, to help inspire the voter-registration drives in that city.

I have tried many times to think of how we could better have used Malcolm's talents. His brand of nationalism was, of course, unacceptable to CORE. But perhaps we too were at fault for not knowing sooner that some form of nationalism, or group-ism or ethnocentrism—there is no suitable name yet for this mood I am trying to describe—can be incorporated into CORE's inner life without fatally compromising its ultimate ideals.

Even Malcolm's theories of violence demand attention. The editorial pages of the nation's liberal newspapers blandly dismiss the Muslims as racists-in-reverse and advise us to banish this inverted Ku Klux Klan from our house. I once heard Malcolm snap at a newspaperman who asked him the differences between the Muslims and the Klan: "We haven't lynched anyone. They've got a lot of years and a lot of blood on us." As callous as that answer may seem, it reflects the way many Negroes think: the white man has been free to murder and maraud for centuries; with impunity he has raped our women and emasculated our sons. We were not even permitted what every other age and society has respected as an apt response—personal revenge. In how many lands would such known murderers as those hundreds who walk Southern streets this very day feel as safe as they do in this country? *Lex talionis* has been with us since the Old Testament, and yet the *very moment* Negroes entertain the same thought that embattled and deeply wronged men have always entertained, the moment we dream all-too-human dreams of revenge or merely of self-defense, we are lumped with the Klan. While I disagree with Malcolm's philosophy, for reasons I shall discuss in a moment, this equation of KKK violence with the Negro's desire to defend himself, it seems to me as it did to Malcolm, shows a monstrous deficiency of moral sense.

Malcolm assumed that where Negroes are concerned, there is no law; that, indeed, the law is a mask for white oppression. This is *often* the case, especially in the South— though I do not believe that it is so often the case as Malcolm did. But certainly it is the case in many places and it has been for long enough to convince some Negroes that it will remain the case, pious professions of good intentions notwithstanding. Actually, Malcolm stated the case for self-defense quite persuasively:

> It is criminal to teach a man not to defend himself when he is the constant victim of brutal attacks. It is legal and lawful to own a shotgun or a rifle. We believe in obeying the law. In areas where our people are the constant victims of brutality, and the government seems unwilling or unable to protect them . . . we should form rifle clubs that can be used to defend our lives and our property in time of emergency. . . . When our people are bitten by dogs they are within their rights to kill those dogs. We should be peaceful, law-abiding . . . but the time has come for the American Negro to fight back in self-defense whenever and wherever he is being unjustly attacked. If the government thinks I am wrong for saying this, then let the government start doing its job.

With much of the doctrine of self-defense stated here I have no objection. There *are* particular and extenuating circumstances in which self-defense is justified and even constitutional. In 1925 Dr. Osian Sweet, a Negro physician living in Detroit, shot a man while defending his newly purchased house from an attacking mob. He was charged with murder, and defended in court by the great Clarence Darrow. The court, presided over by Frank Murphy, later Supreme Court Justice, ruled him not guilty on the ground that a man has the constitutional right to defend his hearth and home. Today, in Jonesboro and Bogalusa, Louisiana, Negro men, for years harassed and terrorized by marauding whites, have organized rifle clubs for self-defense. The Deacons they call themselves. And to my mind conditions there warrant this. I certainly have benefited from the protection the Deacons have provided. The simple fact is that the concept of equal justice and equal protection has broken down in these places, if it ever existed there to begin with, and the law *is* a mask for white oppression.

The danger in Malcolm's doctrine is that it may readily be subverted into an excuse for generalized and indiscriminate violence, generalized and indiscriminate revenge. A War: White vs. Black. I think Malcolm often succumbed to this danger, at least verbally, and many young people under his spell openly advocate a kind of purgative violence. Mostly they just talk and talk. Actually, if these violence-mongers were serious about what they say, they wouldn't say it. They would plan their violence privately and execute it clandestinely, and then brave the consequences. But I suspect many of these men have no heart for that kind of anonymity. They remind me of the "revolutionaries" who announced to the press beforehand that they were going to tie up traffic on the opening day of the World's Fair. They reaped weeks of publicity and also destroyed any chance they had of succeeding. Had they been totally serious, they would have kept their plan quiet. But they were not ultimately serious and neither, I think, was Malcolm.

A good deal has been said about the public appeal, during the 1964 Harlem Riots, by rent-strike organizer Jesse Gray for a hundred men willing to risk death to form a revolutionary militia. Was this not a "serious" advocacy of violence? I was present, and it is interesting to note that the ardor of the crowd dampened considerably when they heard Gray's appeal: very few men volunteered and a paper passed around attracted few names. In other words, when the angry mob was actually confronted with the possibility of engaging in planned violence and pondered its real dangers, almost all were unwilling to go ahead. Whether Gray intended this to happen I do not know. But

I do know that in the midst of the riot few *contemplated* violence.

Serious or not, this constant advocacy of violence can backfire, for the rage it encourages often can be vented only within the Negro community. There is an enormous incidence of senseless violence within the Negro community, and I believe much of it results from such inverted anger. Many said Malcolm's assassination was a case of violent chickens coming home to roost—and whether one agrees with this particular interpretation of the assassination or not,* it is true that Malcolm's death symbolized again the futility and the immorality of violence.

But I think Malcolm's philosophy of violence deserves a second comment. As mistaken and misguided as it may be doctrinally, it has a certain psychological validity. I have mentioned the resentment Negroes feel over the way whites swarm over them with criticism the moment they abandon pure love and merely consider the notion of self-defense. The hypocrisy of this criticism is galling. The Negro sees analogies everywhere. There was silence in the press during the years in which hundreds of thousands of Congolese were being slaughtered; but then there came huge headlines: FIFTY WHITES KILLED IN CONGO. Why not an airlift to Mississippi, they ask? The Negro has been silenced from speaking his mind for centuries, merely speaking, and now many whites are trying to silence him again. Is it any surprise that with the freedom gained in the last years we should now hear in public the angry, preposterous, extravagant and all-too-human talk of revenge that

---

* Gandhi, too, was assassinated—by a Hindu rival. Certainly his assassination was not a case of violence coming home to roost. We should resist the simplistic invitation to interpret Malcolm's death as only a case of poetic justice. Malcolm's killers have not been convicted and I have a hunch the real story of his death will surprise those who saw in it a case of Muslim revenge. Malcolm was warring on the international narcotics interests in Harlem, and they were not pleased about it.

Negroes have been keeping to themselves for centuries? One of the glories of the liberty gained in the last decade is that it has freed Negroes to speak up and talk back to whites. Some have reveled in the opportunity.

After leaving the Muslims, Malcolm mostly talked. He had no program and no stomach for organizing a really effective organization (the organization of Afro-American Unity could not have numbered more than 250 at the time of his death). In part he was the creature of the press and television, which have inflated more than one black reputation with their attention. Yet he was a poet who stirred many a black heart as he stirred mine more than once. One young CORE worker sized up his appeal brilliantly: "I'm sick of all this active non-violence," he said; "I'm going to join Malcolm and get some non-active violence."

Precisely because so much of what he said was so valid psychologically, Malcolm and his heirs have succeeded in discrediting the whole philosophy of non-violence in the eyes of many Negroes. Perhaps we at CORE have failed to show how effective and virile non-violence can be. Medgar Evers, who was murdered in Mississippi, once said to me, "Jim, I must confess that I am not a believer in non-violence." He showed me the gun hidden in his car. Evers never went for a ride without checking under the hood of his car for a bomb. He was followed constantly. On the road at night he would never let another car pass him. I have often wondered whether Evers should have had to apologize to me for wishing to protect himself. We must show that non-violence is something more than turning the other cheek, that it can be aggressive within the limits a civilized order will permit. Where we cannot influence the heart of the evil-doer, we can force an end to the evil practice. Boycotts, picketing, civil disobedience, unflinching courage, and brute persistence are virile enough for any man whose aim is to accomplish something. Even professions of love have a forceful effect at times. Gandhi himself said that he would prefer to see a man resist evil with violence than fail to resist evil out of fear. The choice therefore is not at all between pure love and violence. Between them there are many paths which are psychologically valid and politically effective.

CORE is fully aware of the dangers of nationalism. There are sinister characters lurking in the shadows of the literally hundreds of tiny black nationalist sects which breed in the sprawling black ghettos of our cities. A doctrine of noble martyrdom, which may not be so easily silenced by tactical considerations, is abroad. "The black man, having had enough, is prepared to die so that he may not live as a dog. . . . Ours may well be the sacrificed generation," writes the magazine *Liberator*. This counsel could take hold. Martyrdom can be heady wine for young men and women who feel they have nothing to live for anyway. Unquestionably, Chinese-style Communists and professional revolutionaries of other stripes are seeking to capitalize on nationalist sentiment in the ghetto. And they will try to set the Negroes to fighting the "Yankee imperialists" at home as their black brothers will be said to be fighting them abroad. Their appeal is potent: "Join us in the world-wide struggle of black against white. In America you are a minority; in the world we are by far the majority. History is on our side. The white imperialist must be crushed and you must help shoulder the burden. Perhaps you will not see the triumph of the black man in your lifetime, but you cannot honorably desist from playing your role. History will honor your efforts." Today there are very few Negro Communists and Negroes historically have frustrated every attempt to infiltrate their ranks. CORE itself closes membership to Communists. But if foreign

affairs should be dominated by news of racial warfare and
the great mass of people now swarming hopelessly in the
ghetto are convinced that our system holds no hope for
them, the dangers from the nationalist organizations infiltrated and influenced by Chinese-style Communists will
increase.

I do not wish to be misunderstood on this point. I think
there is a danger from Chinese-style Communists—Maoists
working through black nationalist organizations in the
North. But I do not wish this statement linked with the
casual charge one hears more and more often today—
that the civil rights movement, particularly in the South, is
"Communist infiltrated." With regard to the South and the
civil rights movement there (the black nationalists are in
the North and are *not* part of the civil rights movement),
the charge is a red herring.

What lessons has CORE learned from these reflections?
First of all, it is clear that we must not, we cannot, leave
the ghetto to the rabid nationalists. For it is in the urban
ghetto that Negro history will be made in the forseeable
future. In the last thirty years millions of Negroes have
moved into the great cities of the North, and more and
more are moving to those cities of the South which soon
will be more urban than Southern. Today more than 60
per cent of America's twenty million Negroes live in large
cities and about 40 per cent live in fifteen great Northern
cities. All trends indicate that the urbanization of the Negro will continue. By 1975 Negroes may constitute a majority or near majority of the populations of several major
cities: Detroit, Chicago, Philadelphia, Newark. The average inhabitant of these vast black pockets will be uneducated, untrained, and often, unemployed. Of those who are
employed, many will be performing the most low-paying
and life-sapping labor. Indeed, we are creating a massive

under class of black men ill-suited temperamentally and materially for life in this cybernetic society. Today, about 55 per cent of Negro youth from eighteen to twenty-five years of age are school dropouts. Even if we can miraculously redeem unborn generations, there is the present one which faces a desperately hard future. There *have* been great gains in job opportunities and educational opportunities for Negroes over the last few years, and with organizations like CORE maintaining vigilance and demanding justice, these opportunities will continue to expand apace. But we can no longer evade the knowledge that *most* Negroes will not be helped by equal opportunity. These are staggering problems for which the traditional CORE program of anti-discrimination is ill-equipped. We are seeking new techniques and emphases.

Politically, the potential power of the ghetto is enormous; we have dropped CORE's traditional neutrality with regard to politics, and now must organize the Negro community, house by house, block by block, into political units. There will be hundreds of neighborhood associations, apartment house councils, block committees; between these small units we must begin to forge larger alliances. We must engage in political education, demonstrating to people in the ghetto that there are connections between the local demand for a new traffic light or a rat-extermination campaign and the larger demands for public-works programs and stiffer civil rights legislation. At all times we must serve the people and let them govern their own activities. As the Muslims did, we must enter pool halls and reeking tenements, looking for new leaders and followers. We must begin, in short, to shape an articulate sense of communal aspiration among the black masses and bring to the ghetto CORE's conviction that the people can help themselves.

Economically, we will urge a variety of self-help programs. In Chicago, a CORE project organized unemployed Negro youth in a slum-clean-up campaign. We then went to City Hall and left a bill enumerating the costs of the effort—as it were, doing public works before they were authorized. The bill was unpaid but an important example to other Negro communities was set. There are a thousand tasks to be done in the community which are thoroughly within the capacities of the unskilled workers. Then, too, CORE has plans to organize food co-ops, credit unions; we will encourage small businesses by providing expert advice and perhaps even some financial backing. We can even seek to develop larger businesses and industries in the community. In Boston CORE has compiled a list of Negro builders and set about getting work for them; this technique has great possibilities. Another important task will be to train aspiring plumbers and carpenters and the like to take the tests which lead to the apprenticeship programs. Many talented youngsters simply do not know how to take tests. These are only a few possible ideas. We will set ourselves to developing others.

There is also a great need for remedial education services and job training. Much of the money for this will be coming from such government programs as the War on Poverty and from private foundations. It is crucial that this money be distributed by the community through its own channels. The government could very well commit the errors of the welfare agencies, tending to free people rather than empowering them to free themselves. But with our political arm we can help persuade the government to provide the people with the services they demand and need, and dissuade it from telling them what they *should* demand and need. The government could very well be persuaded to underwrite new growth and healthy development in Negro community life. It could also nip that growth in the bud by unwise efforts.

Finally, there is cultural work to be done, and this is perhaps most basic of all. Like the nationalists, we must try to conquer the Negro sense of inferiority. We feel this will be possible only when it is legitimate to be a black man in this country. And here CORE has a unique contribution to make. *CORE knows that Negro identity will emerge only in the midst of purposive and realistic effort in America. The Nationalists offer doctrine. We must offer program as well.* The nationalists talk and harangue—their radical anger breeds radical and foolish thoughts—because they are doing nothing; they have no stake in the world, no stake in the land, and hence, little hope. This dissociated situation breeds only bravado. I believe there is some psychological validity in what they say. There is also a great potentiality for destructiveness. With no real work to do in America, their advice to love blacks turns into a program to hate whites. Eager to act manfully, they can only imagine petty schemes of violence and revenge. CORE must get the Negro community to work on itself and on America. With its proven techniques of non-violent direct action, it must inject Negro activity into the political life of the community. It must teach Negroes to act upon America in America in the presence of Americans. It must begin the great task of redefining nationalism and redefining integration, so that we can incorporate proud black men and self-assertive black communities as legitimate partners in a new America. There is much to be discussed: What is the Negro's proper relationship with Africa? Should the Negro work within the two-party system? What is the future of the integration program? There are no easy answers to these questions. I think examination will show them to be very similar to questions other Americans have asked in this land. And part of the challenge of being black and American in the next few years will be in seeking answers.

5

INTEGRATION OR DESEGREGATION

One feels his two-ness—An American, a Negro, two souls, two thoughts, two unreconciled strivings, two warring ideals, in one dark body. . . .

The history of the American Negro is the history of this strife—this longing to attain self-conscious manhood, to merge his double self into a better and truer self. . . . He would not Africanize America, for America has too much to teach the world and Africa. He would not bleach the Negro soul in a flood of white Americanism, for he knows that Negro blood has a message for the world. He simply wishes to make it possible for a man to be both a Negro and an American without being cursed and spit upon. . . .

—W. E. B. DU BOIS, 1903

No word has served to epitomize the movement's goals for these last ten years as well as "integration." We would be integrated into America and destroy "segregation," the hated opposite of this new concept. So we demanded integrated schools and housing and employment, and integrated commercial messages on television, and integrated casts on opera and dramatic stages, and integrated movies, and mayors' committees, and civic-planning boards, etc. The value of integration took on the status of a self-evident truth.

Today, however, many Negroes, gripped by a new wave of self-pride and group-pride, are beginning to ask critical questions of the integrationist creed: How can we be prideful without advocating an inverted form of "separate but equal"? Is self-pride another term for self-segregation? Must we renounce ourselves and our community for the sake of integration?

Let me say immediately that much of "integration" remains valid for us and, in our view, for America, but with somewhat altered emphasis and meaning.

What do we mean by "integration"? For some the term means complete assimilation, a kind of random dispersal of Negroes throughout the society and the economy. There would be no Negro neighborhoods, no Negro schools, no jobs reserved for Negroes. America would be a land of individuals who were American and nothing else, and Negro individuals would differ from their fellow Americans only in their skin color—that most insignificant of human differences. Some of us even dreamed that differences of color too would soon melt away when love and colorblindness permeated the land. As I have said, no one can question the ultimate goodness of this ideal. The question is: Is it too good to be true?

Integration has been the nation's implicit ideal since America was a glint in Jefferson's eye. It is nothing but Jeffersonian individualism extended to all people. But it did not become a practical political goal until quite recently, and the reasons for this make an important story. Like most Americans, Negroes were still accepting "separate but equal" as the law of the land as late as the mid-forties, and our major efforts were expended in making the "equal" of "separate but equal" a reality. In the decades before the 1954 Supreme Court decision desegregating schools the NAACP brought to the court cases treating discrimination in education, voting, interstate and intrastate travel, public facilities, and selection of juries. The court in those years invariably found that Negro facilities were palpably unequal and ruled that segregation was constitutional only if facilities and accommodations were truly equal. In other words, the whole burden of the civil rights movement's case then was: if facilities are going to be separate, at least make them equal. Separate but equal was reaffirmed.

Toward the end of the forties NAACP lawyers and strategists began to argue that in certain respects separate facilities could never be equal. For example, a Negro relegated to a Negro law school could not hope to make professional contacts that would enable him to swim in the main stream of the profession as readily as someone at a white law school—and this was true no matter how beautiful the buildings and how well-stocked the library at the Negro law school was. A Pullman seat in a car reserved for Negroes could not be the equal of a seat in the white car because the manifest intention of "for Negroes only" was to convey inferiority. By a natural process of evolution the demand for what we might term equal-if-separate turned into a demand for desegregation.

To argue that a beautiful Negro law school or a plush seat in a Negro Pullman was inferior to its white counterpart demanded some subtlety. To argue that the segregated public school system treated Negroes as second-class citizens demanded no subtlety at all. Comparison of expenditures per student, school plant, teachers' salaries, experience and training of teachers, books and supplies, and other measurable factors, made it clear that throughout the country, and in the South particularly, the Negro, forced by law and fact into segregated schools, was being deprived of equality under law. The 1954 Supreme Court decision attempted to correct this intolerable inequity in the only way practical and intelligent men could—by eliminating the dual school systems.

But the court added a theoretical dimension to its factual and practical findings: "Separate educational facilities," it said, "are *inherently* unequal" [emphasis added] and it cited as evidence certain psychological data—principally those of Professor Kenneth Clark—which document the serious psychological damage race separation causes in Negro youngsters. Now, I am not certain what "inherently unequal" or even "separate educational facilities" mean in this context, and I will want to return to these phrases shortly; but first I would like to explain how we interpreted the court's decision. For us it was a recognition of what every Negro knows: that the system of segregation was mounted and perpetuated for the purpose of keeping the black man down; that it was and is a conspiracy to instill in the Negro *and the white* a sense of Negro inferiority. Segregation is slavery made legal. Segregation *means* inferiority, as indelibly as the scarlet letter meant adulteress to the New England Puritans. The Negro knows this; it was intended that he know this, and so too must any American with the most rudimentary sense of history know it. And now the court was saying that this country would segregate no more. So we began to protest against segregated schools of all kinds, *de facto* and *de jure*, demanding quality integrated education, knowing all the time that we were combating and helping eliminate the hated *meaning* which had been assigned to our lives.

As separate schools were inferior, so too were separate neighborhoods (quite obviously the *meaning* of segregated neighborhoods is simply that the great white world doesn't want black folk living next to it; anyone who doubts this need only observe the hysteria and violence which ensue when a Negro family moves into a white neighborhood). The effect of living in an enforced ghetto is conveyed graphically in the desolation and wreckage, human and material, in which most Negroes live today. So we moved to desegregate housing and some aimed at dismantling the ghetto.

Indeed, every instance and symbol of segregation and every invidious discrimination could now be legitimately challenged. There are millions, and we took them on one by one, case by case. At lunch counters, restaurants, rest rooms, swimming pools, amusement parks, beaches, labor unions, banks, factories, offices, department stores, professional societies, churches, colleges. To the most rabid integrationists even the institutions of Negro communal life were implicated. They saw no reason for a Negro Medical Society; all energies must be directed to breaking down the AMA. Negro colleges, Negro churches, Negro newspapers were at best tolerated as unnecessary anachronisms.

Integration was a white man's cause as well as a black man's, and the literally thousands of interracial organizations which came into being to fight the good fight became themselves temporary models of integrated living. CORE was one, and remains one. Many whites recognize the superiority complex demanded of the white man in a segregated system to be as harmful in its way as the inferiority complex demanded of Negroes. Many quite sincerely set about curing themselves and their neighborhoods and schools of this affliction.

The rabid integrationist aims at mixing every unit of society in "ideal" proportions. In middle-class neighborhoods housing committees were formed to persuade reluctant white homeowners to accept respectable Negroes, and courageous and well-to-do Negroes were sought who would brave white wrath. And when one or two Negroes had entered a neighborhood, the same committees, now with the eager help of the Negroes, organized to keep other Negroes out. We mustn't let the neighborhood tip, they said. Housing developments adopted informal quotas to help engineer integrated living. Dedicated builders, like Morris Milgrim of Philadelphia, began to persuade investors that quality housing projects, open to all, could return a modest profit, and integrated oases soon sprang up in several previously all-white deserts. Many liberals grew uncomfortable with the irony that in order to achieve integration they had to adopt racial quotas of various sorts, designating Negroes in order to eliminate racial designations, as it were, and some became discouraged at the solemn spectacle of Negroes chasing whites from suburb to suburb—in quest of integration. But among white liberals and some black liberals the dream of complete integration persisted.

Almost imperceptibly the demand for desegregation had shaded into a demand for black dispersal and assimilation. We were told, and for a while told ourselves, that *all* Negro separation was inherently inferior, and some folk began to think that Negroes couldn't be fully human in the presence of other Negroes. But what of Africa? Was separation inferior there too? And what of the *de facto* separation of other minority groups, the Jews and Chinese, for example. Was separation so self-evidently inferior for them as it was for us?

I am not a lawyer, but I think that the phrase "separate educational facilities are inherently unequal," which supports the philosophy of total integration, invites some misinterpretation. Separation need not be inferior in all cases and all places. What is crucial is the *meaning* the culture places upon the separation. Separation, in other words, is not necessarily segregation, *though in America, Negro separation in fact and in law means segregation.* This is the crucial insight. The separation of Negroes in America *means* segregation—slavery. In its decision the Supreme Court was offering a particular and indisputable reading of the meaning of American history. In the context of our civilization with its history of racism, the court said, separate educational institutions are inherently inferior.

When a Negro child goes through the doors of a segregated school, he knows implicitly that his culture is telling

him to go there because he is not fit to be with others, and
every time a Negro child hears of a white parent who becomes hysterical at the thought that his child will have to
endure the likes of him, he feels the pressure of his inferiority a little more firmly. As a result he is damaged. And this
too the Supreme Court saw. As long as the ideology of racial inferiority and superiority persists, segregation will be
an insult and blackness a stigma.

One does not undo the accumulated meanings of centuries by waving a magic wand: "*Abracadabra!* Once you
were segregation. Now you are separation." This is tokenism: the belief that by one gesture, one concession, yes,
even one sincere cry of the heart, one moment of honest
compassion, the country will transform the manifest meaning of historic life-ways. The desegregation fight is crucial
to all Americans. What we are attempting is nothing less
than to reverse the latent *meaning* of our lives and practices. For a civilization to do this takes remarkable strength
of purpose, time, persistence, and most of all, honesty. Because the foot is on his neck, Negroes have been much more
honest about America than the whites. We know this civilization is still segregated in its heart of hearts. We test the
spirit of its ways, and white Americans who would be
honest about America listen attentively when we tell them
about their country.

Now, this distinction between separation and segregation was often made by Malcolm X. Time and again, he
denied that the Black Muslims were segregationists. We
are separationists, he said, not segregationists. Without
qualification all American Negroes hate segregation. Some
Negroes, however, would *choose* to live separately, and
Malcolm saw this and tried to make it a *legitimate* desire.
But in one very essential respect I differ strongly with Malcolm. He believed that Negroes can change the manifest

meaning of their separated existence solely by the force of their own wills. I believe that there is much Negroes can do for themselves, but I do not believe they can separate truly if the nation does not simultaneously desegregate.

Culturally we are Americans, and like all men we know ourselves, in part, by what our culture tells us about ourselves. The fact is that American segregationists take delight in the Black Muslims' program. I do not believe the rumor that the Ku Klux Klan and some Texas millionaires support the Muslims, but I do know that they take no small comfort from Muslim activities. Even CORE's decision to emphasize self-help in the Negro community succeeds in making Parents and Taxpayers Associations breathe easier. And Negroes know this. In other words, there is a certain validity to the integrationist insight that separate Negro efforts and institutions simply perpetuate segregation. If, in his heart of hearts, the Negro believes that self-separation is only a rationalization for cowardly acceptance of segregation, then separation will fail.

The only way Negro separation would not mean segregation is if the Negro has the sense that he chooses to live separately, and this will happen only when total freedom of choice is a reality in America. Desegregation and the development of Negro self-pride work side by side. Desegregation makes separation possible. *

What we wish is the freedom of choice which will cause any choice we make to seem truly our own. That freedom of choice must apply throughout American society and American life. A person should be able to choose where he wants to live and live there. If he chooses to live in Lovely Lane in Orchard Gardens, he should be able to, if he has the money to swing it. He should be able to work at any

---

* Of course, Negroes do not have the right to exclude whites who choose to live among them.

job for which he is qualified and equipped, regardless of
his color. Jim Brown, a thoughtful man and pretty good
fullback, offended some people when he said that he personally wouldn't want to live with whites but that he
damned well wanted to know that he could if he did want
to. I think he represents the thinking of many Negroes.

But many other Negroes will choose to integrate; they
should be permitted to. James Baldwin asks whether it is
worth integrating into a sinking ship. Many middle-class
Negroes, whose spines are straighter than Baldwin and others suppose, would answer, "You're damned right it is."
Many will buy their twenty- or thirty-thousand-dollar
homes and move into neighborhoods which suit them culturally and financially. Indeed, most Negroes integrating
such a neighborhood will probably have a higher educational level than their white neighbors, prejudice being
what it is. It is easy to scoff at the spectacle of a middle-
class Negro shoving his way into a white enclave. Some
say, "Does white approval mean that much? Why go
where you're not wanted?" But I have known many of
these men. They brave abuse nobly and stand tough witness to noble ideals. Their acts shake the system of segregation and for that reason their efforts are more closely
connected to efforts to eliminate the psychological ghetto
than is commonly granted.

We must not forget that there are solid, perhaps incom-
parable, values in truly integrated living. W. E. B. Du Bois,
a proud black man, once said that the real tragedy in our
world today is not that men are poor; all men know something of poverty. Nor that men are ignorant; what is
truth? Nor that men are wicked; who is good? But that
men know so little of men.

It is important for Negroes to know white men and for
white men to know Negroes. I might add that white men

should insist that we live among them for their own sakes. And if some Negroes resist white blandishments, they will be fuller men for having resisted a valuable temptation.

Those who glibly abuse "middle-class" Negroes often commit the racist fallacy of demanding that black men behave according to their definition of him. If a black man wants to skip five thousand lunches, as Dick Gregory says, in order to buy a Cadillac, then he should. At CORE we have come to believe that in a free society many Negroes will choose to live and work separately, *although not in total isolation.* They will cultivate the pride in themselves which comes in part from their efforts to make this a free land. Even those living and working in "racially balanced" situations will value their Negro identity more than before. In helping themselves, they will come to love themselves. From loving themselves, they will determine to help themselves. They will be Americans and Negroes. They will be free to pick and choose from several rich traditions. They may thrill to the example of modern Africa and search out the richness of Africa's past as Du Bois did. Or they may as Americans and Westerners seize as models such great American cultural heroes as Lincoln or Hemingway or Duke Ellington. They will be as American as St. Patrick's Day and Columbus Day and Rosh Hashanah.

We are beginning now to see a more ideal division of effort within CORE and among the groups comprising the entire civil rights movement. Clearly the desegregation movement must continue unabated. We must demand that segregation end. Tokenism of all kinds must be rejected. We shall demand quality integrated education, now definitely adding to it the demand that Negro history be taught in the public schools so that our youngsters can learn that they are ancient citizens of this land. There must be open housing and fair employment practices, in law and in fact. And we will still demand preferential, compensatory treatment (I shall discuss this more fully later). In brief, there should be no abatement in the efforts of the last years. At the same time we will enter the Negro community, working with those masses who couldn't care less about integrating and couldn't afford it if they did care. Our efforts in the ghettos to help the people build a community life and a community spirit will be spurred by the knowledge that desegregation is taking place simultaneously. In this way segregation will be transformed into separation. Perhaps "independence" is a better term than separation. We shall become independent men. We will accept, in other words, part of Malcolm's insight that segregation will become separation only with a separate effort of Negro heart and soul rejecting the notion of some of the older civil rights organizations (and of the original CORE) that desegregation and integration *in itself* will accomplish miracles. But we will correct the Muslims' belief that the Negro can do all things alone. There must be simultaneous desegregation and we must demand it. By this amendment we will affirm that we are Americans and that the civil rights movement is an American movement.

It is clear from this summary that there is something for everyone to do. How often I have been asked by white middle-class liberals, "But what can I do?" The answer is simple. You can integrate your neighborhoods and schools as purely and diligently as ever. You are responsible for segregation and only you can end it. The white man should be an integrationist. And the fact that some Negroes now build their own lives independently without apology has no bearing upon this white responsibility. Nor, I think, should whites advise Negroes to separate themselves, for

that always sounds suspiciously like a demand for segregation. Separation, independence, must be our choice to make
and our program to achieve. It should affect the traditional
integrationist efforts of civil rights and civil liberties groups,
church and labor groups, fair housing and fair employment
committees not a jot.

Is it divisive of me to suggest that all parties to the movement will not share identical perspectives? Some think so.
But I believe that one cannot be all men at all times and
remain himself. There is a two-ness, to use Du Bois's term,
in the movement as there is in the Negro, and no synthesis,
as far as I can see now, is possible. Perhaps ultimately, God
willing. We should not be frightened by slight ambiva-
lences. They are a sign that we are becoming free, for
freedom eludes simple definitions.

I I

We might now look into two sensitive issues. One has
been urgently debated for several years; the other is relegated to a limbo of silence, perhaps out of fear of the
repercussions open advocacy would cause. I speak of our
demands for special, "preferential," compensatory treatment for Negroes and, of course, of interracial marriage.

Admittedly there is something startling about any demand that a whole ethnic group receive special attention.
It seems to go in the teeth of our belief in individual fair
play. "Are all Negroes disadvantaged?" critics ask. "Should
we assume that a black skin is itself sufficient proof that the
bearer deserves special consideration?" When other "mi-
norities" devised a strategy to get a fair shake, they were
"content"—the argument against us goes—to achieve immunity as individuals from group discrimination. Indeed,

Negro organizations have been partners for years in a broad civil rights alliance which produced legislation in many Northern states attempting to establish non-discriminatory employment and home occupancy and in general seeking to obtain equal opportunity for all individuals (I say "attempting," because the states have moved to execute these laws with the speed of a glacier). So when an organization like CORE or Urban League demands special group attention—in education, job training, and employment—many sense a thief afoot in the liberal house, trying to steal advantages he doesn't individually deserve.

Now, as I have pointed out, the aim of treating each individual as an individual and nothing more—which is the premise underlying the philosphy of integration—is undeniably sound. The idea is to give everyone an equal start for equal opportunities. But the simple truth is that the Negro does not start on the same line as whites, nor is the economy he enters today the same as that which the immigrants entered—individually, they say—over the last half century.

The reasons for this are historical and have to do, as I have said, with the meaning and impact of segregation. But the fact of it is crystal clear. Tom Kahn, Executive Secretary of the League for Industrial Democracy, has graphically described the economics of American racism in *The Economics of Equality*. The median income of Negro families, says Kahn, is $3,233—54 per cent of the white family's median income. And in the last ten years the Negro's position, relative to the white, has actually declined. Unemployment is twice as high among Negroes as among whites, and among the young, eighteen to twenty-six years old, the disproportion is far greater. Ominously, most of the job classifications in which Negro participation has increased in the last decade are in those unskilled and semi-skilled areas which are today being eliminated by automation and cybernetics. Considering how poorly the Negro is being educated today in comparison to whites (who aren't being educated too well either) and considering the skills and training which more than ever will be necessary in the new economy, we can confidently predict that Negro unemployment and general economic depression will increase in the coming years. Unless something is done about it.

It is cruel nonsense in this new mass age of super technology to speak of equal opportunity in individualistic terms; the back wheels of the car never catch the front. The Negro community constitutes an economic disaster area. And it was with this in mind that CORE supported the Urban League's call for a domestic Marshall Plan which would offer the same kind of special and concerted attention in employment, education, and welfare that America gave to Hungarian and Cuban refugees, or that we gave to the G.I. after World War II, or that we give to Appalachia today.

We recommend a crash program in education and in job training, stressing that the Negro be trained to enter the new technological economy. We emphasized that he be trained in these emerging job categories because there is some tendency in technical high schools and some of the programs developed in the anti-poverty program to train the Negro for jobs which are either nonexistent or fast disappearing from the economy. And we recommend this to all institutions and agencies in American life—government (federal, state, and local) as well as private corporations, businesses, labor unions, and service organizations.*

* In some respects the Urban League and CORE place different emphasis on various aspects of compensation. The ten-point program which

It is important to emphasize that we make these recommendations not only in the name of equity but in the name of historical justice. The integrationists fear that by demanding special help for the Negro, we will make him more Negro than ever and compound his disabilities. It is a class problem, they will say, not a race problem. Well, it is that too. But we must call injustice by its given name. America is racist and it is a man called Negro who is specially victimized beyond his class and beyond any other formal classifications one might coin. And he knows he is. He will not cease to be victimized nor will he cease to victimize himself until segregation of mind and spirit ends. And to end segregation this nation must turn directly to the Negro and undo what it has done. We are not so worried if we get to be known as Negroes in the process. We rather like the name these days. Again, we are desegregationists, not necessarily integrationists.

As for interracial marriage, it is, of course, the touchiest of subjects. Perhaps, as James Baldwin and others have finally said, *sex* is at the bottom of the race problem. Well we know how irrepressibly those dreadful words drift to the lips of whites: "Would you want your daughter. . . ." In ten years the civil rights movement has forced this nation to tear down numerous symbols of Negro deg-

---

Whitney Young formulated in 1963 centers its fire on the business community—corporations and foundations. While we second Young's motion —and are grateful that he is so influential with American businessmen —we have worked on smaller units in the economy: labor unions, small and middle-sized businesses. Both Urban League and CORE have pressed for vigorous and expensive government programs.

I think it should be pointed out, too, that in some degree our demands for special attention have been fully accepted and applied—albeit under a different rubric. Opportunities for talented and obviously promising young Negroes to attend choice universities and get lucrative and satisfying work have increased markedly. Unfortunately, these opportunities are still reserved for a talented twentieth of our people. We must now apply our special effort where it is most needed.

radation: separate waiting rooms and rest rooms; separate laws and regulations; separate gestures; separate vocabulary and manners—we challenged them all. And yet we have tiptoed around what a man from Mars might objectively call the most degrading and revealingly racist symbols of American public life. As I write this some nineteen states, mainly in the South, have "anti-miscegenation laws," prohibiting marriage between the races. In these states, even those "mixed" couples which have legally married in other states cannot live or even travel together as man and wife. Constitutional lawyers tell me that these statutes are indubitably unconstitutional, and though in 1965 the Supreme Court was preparing to rule on these laws, it is still a fact of history, to be recorded, that until recently the court, with full permission of our Negro organizations, has avoided the issue. Jewish friends tell me that the first clue of what was to happen in Germany was the infamous Nuremberg Laws prohibiting sexual intercourse between Aryans and Jews. From that brutish moment, they say, all things followed. Yet we have had Nuremberg Laws for almost a century here. And remained silent.

We Negroes have made something of an art of detecting hypocrisy lately, yet what hypocrisy is so overt as this one? As Lillian Smith has shown so eloquently in *Killers of the Dream*, and as any Negro anywhere knows, Southerners do not believe in sexual segregation; they believe in sexual exploitation. In no respect are we so exploited as in this. Black women are for white men to have; white women are for no one to have. In a typical Southern town, every Negro knows of the whites who are kin to him. Miscegenation, so-called, is an established practice, in one direction. But the Negro male in the South cannot look upon a white woman or even seem to be looking upon her without literally inviting slaughter. And we know it. And in the law it says in effect that we are not fit to be loved in the light of day.*

And yet how tenderly we have treated this issue. Reasons are not difficult to cite. Clearly, we cannot even broach the topic without throwing whites into apoplectic resistance. Why risk losing other goals? How do you say to people who are literally insane on the subject, "We are not advocating anything, we are only saying the prohibition is insulting"?

And we are *not* advocating interracial marriage. I believe that such advocacy is as dirty-minded as the prohibition. One simply must not dictate to the human heart this way. (As Eleanor Roosevelt said, marriage is not a social matter with private implications, it is a private matter with social implications.) Those few who advocate amalgamation and those who would prohibit it—as many black nationalists would—are equally guilty of tampering. All we can do is try to make men believe they are free by leaving them to their choices.

Should I now rush, as many commentators do, to assure the reader that interracial marriage couldn't be further from the mind of most Negroes? Indeed, from the description of growing pride in the Negro community which I have offered in this book, many may draw this conclusion. If I were asked, Do you expect a significant increase in interracial marriages as desegregation progresses? I would answer: No, I do not foresee a significant increase. Asked if I believe in such marriages, I would answer that what I believe or what anyone believes should not matter. Free men who care about the freedom of others should keep their counsel in these matters.

* A young Negro was convicted in North Carolina a while back for "reckless eyeballing." "Rape by leer" was another term used to describe this "crime."

CORE will not make an issue of the question, and that itself is something of a commentary on this country. We are normally a fairly aggressive bunch. Yet in our hearts we know that desegregation will not be complete until America is cleansed of the filth of legislating whom one may not marry.

6

AFRICA REVISITED

WHEN freedom comes,
the Negro, like members of other ethnic groups, will
have an important role in the determination and definition
of American foreign policy. Just as those of Jewish, Irish,
German, Polish, or English lineage fashion their sense of
what is right for America out of their particular memories
and foreign attachments, so too will the Negro now force
America to deal honorably with *his* kin, *his* special foreign
interest: Africa. We are twenty-two million strong, more
numerous than others who are far more influential than
we. And we will not be free until the nation answers to
our sense of the American world mission as responsively
as it has answered to other citizens'. It is as an exercise of
citizenship, then, and as a token of what America can expect from her black citizens in the future, that I offer
these notes and reflections on a trip to Africa.*

* Much has happened in Africa since this chapter was written: Tshombe
is out and Kasavubu is wetting his feet in the African mainstream. And

I

Until a few years ago, roughly the time that the Gold
Coast became Ghana, the mass of American Negroes had
little knowledge of Africa. Scholars like W. E. B. Du Bois
and Rayford Logan had written about Africa, of course,
and there were recurrent "back to Africa" fads in the ghetto,
but for the most part we held, like other Americans, a
Hollywood stereotype of the dark continent: half-naked
black savages dancing around a boiling pot of missionary
soup. I remember very clearly in my childhood, in Texas,
my buddy and I would go down to the movie house every
Saturday afternoon and watch the Tarzan movies. And when
those scenes of Africans dancing around the pot came on,
I would elbow him and say, "That's you, Irving." His response always was, "No, man, that ain't me. I didn't come
from Africa."

Attitudes first began to change around 1954, with the
first visit of Haile Selassie to this country. Could this show
of regal pomp and dignity represent Africa? Characteristi-
cally, the press in this country went to great pains to point
out that while Ethiopia was technically in Africa, Haile
Selassie was not a Negro. Really, Ethiopians were Semitic
folk or Hamitic peoples, not Negroid, the implication being that American Negroes should take no pride from
Ethiopia. Then Ghana became independent and other
black nations fought successfully for independence. We
saw proud black people representing these nations in the
councils of the United Nations, appearing on television,

the white minority in Rhodesia threatens the peace of the world. Events
compound events so quickly that any updating of these observations
would be outdated before it is done. I have therefore elected to keep intact these reflections on Africa, which were written soon after my return
in February, 1965.

writing articles, speaking fluent English and French. We were impressed. Cultural groups soon began to form all over the country, calling themselves Afro-American, studying African art, African dance, African history.

It is no accident, in my judgment, that the emergence of the new nations of Africa coincided with the emergence of the civil rights revolution in the United States. Men who would make history must have a history. As the civil rights revolution got rolling, it became essential that we locate ourselves within the total saga of mankind, telling of our role in the great story.

Because of these developments, several of us in the civil rights movement—A. Philip Randolph, Dorothy Height (President of the National Council of Negro Women), Whitney Young, Jr., Roy Wilkins, Martin Luther King, and I—began to think about establishing closer liaison between the African revolutions and the civil rights revolution. As Americans of African descent, we felt we should take the lead in interpreting for America what was happening in Africa and also in explaining to Africans what was happening in America. We felt too that our opinions should weigh in the formation of American foreign policy regarding Africa. And it was out of these considerations that the American Negro Leadership Conference on Africa was formed in 1962. In late 1964 the conference received a grant from the American Society of African Culture to finance an extended trip to Africa. They asked me to represent them; I accepted eagerly.*

This was my second trip to Africa. My first, six years earlier, had been an overwhelming, an almost religious experience, which had taken me completely by surprise. I was working for a trade union then. Before I left, one of

* I was accompanied on the entire trip, except for the Congo, by James Baker of the American Society of African Culture.

my shop stewards came to me and said, "Jim, I hear you're going to Africa; take this bottle and fill it with water from the River Nile and bring it back to me." Another shop steward thrust a small wooden box into my hand and said, "Jim, when you get to Africa, fill this box with African soil and bring it home for me and I'll plant a flower in it." And my father, whom I never knew as a sentimental man— he was an Old Testament and Hebrew scholar—said, when he heard I was going to Africa, "Son, I hear you're going home; well, when you get there, go to West Africa, look up my relatives, tell them that I said hello, and that I'm doing well." I could not have predicted such comments from these men in a million years. When I landed in Africa, I felt quite literally like falling on my knees and kissing the earth. Like most American Negroes I know nothing of my family beyond my grandparents. What section of Africa had they come from, which tribe? I searched faces for some sign, though I knew it was fruitless. Yet all over Africa black men made me feel as if *they* were my family. When I left Nigeria, on that first visit, Nigerian trade-unionists gathered at the airport to see me off, and they threw their arms around me and kissed me. A woman came up to me—I had told them about my friend giving me a bottle to fill with water from the Nile—and she thrust a bottle filled with water into my hand. I had no idea where it came from, but she said, "Take home this water from the River Nile." And another woman thrust into my hand not a box but a handkerchief filled with dirt. And others said, "Dear brother, when you return to America, tell *our* relatives that we are faring well, and tell them to come home."

My second visit was nothing like that at all. During that first visit I had, as Langston Hughes put it, "viewed Africa through the thick mist of race." On the second visit I was less emotional. I could see more dispassionately and rationally—the flaws, the frailties, the power plays, the cruelty, the evil, and the goodness and kindness. Where once Africans had seemed like demigods to me, now they were human, and I found that my sense of kinship could well survive this deflation. Not the mystique of race, but the simple fact of our consonant striving and linked destinies impressed me most. I believe the manner in which the civil rights movement had thrust me into real affairs with tangible prospects had something to do with my change of attitude.

My second trip covered five weeks and nine countries: Tanzania, Kenya, Uganda, Zambia, Southern Rhodesia, Ethiopia, Nigeria, the Congo, and Ghana. I saw the heads of state in practically every country: Julius Nyerere and his two vice-presidents, Karume and Kawawa, in Tanzania; President Kenneth Kaunda in Zambia; President Jomo Kenyatta in Kenya; His Imperial Majesty Haile Selassie I in Ethiopia; President Nnamde Azikiwe in Nigeria; Moise Tshombe and Joseph Kasavubu in the Congo; President Kwame Nkrumah in Ghana. In every country I met with cabinet ministers, members of parliament, and university students. I lectured at universities in several countries and spoke at meetings sponsored by social and civic organizations. And I met with trade-unionists.

II

There is a school of realists in this country who claim that the opinions foreign peoples hold of America are and ought to be irrelevant to the making of our foreign policy. The immorality of such hard-boiled thoughts aside (our actions affect these people and only an immoral man completely ignores the consequences of his acts), they also constitute a poor realism, for the realist would predict the consequences of policy, and what people think of America will show up in their reactions to our policy. And this is especially true of Africa, where the social structure and the structure of opinion are less complex than in America and more likely to reflect national policy. So for realists and moralists alike, I inquired into the whys and wherefores of African attitudes toward America.

I was quite surprised at the extent to which the late President Kennedy was admired in Africa. I am told that in country after country radio and TV announcers broke down in tears before finishing announcements of his assassination. Jomo Kenyatta said, "We understood that young man. He was with us." Why this affection for a man Africans knew only in the image he projected to world opinion? The answer, I concluded, was that as Kennedy was young, so were the Africans, and he appealed to their youth. The "New Frontier" rhetoric matched theirs perfectly. He took over a government at the very moment they did, and with nothing in their experience to teach them that our traditions limit the powers of a President to make the world over according to his dreams, they supposed that he would use American power to implement his high-sounding rhetoric.

Africans believe that after Kennedy's death something fundamental changed in American policy. President Johnson is a shadowy figure to them and they were cautious in accepting my own statements that Johnson identifies with the American Negro much more than Kennedy did. President Nyerere of Tanzania suggested that Vice-President Humphrey tour Africa and especially East Africa to reestablish the emotional ties of Africans with America, and though Tanzania's views may have changed since the recent visit of Mao Tse-tung, I think Nyerere's idea is sound.

Opinions of America vary, of course, from country to

country, but I found the consensus in the East African countries—Tanzania, Uganda, and Kenya—was that America has allied herself with the most reactionary forces on the African continent and that she invariably lines up on the side that is resisting the aspirations of Africans and their leadership. This is the attitude of the man in the street as well as the leaders.

On three issues feeling is particularly bitter. (1) With regard to the Congo, the feeling is that the United States, in league with Belgium, Portugal, Southern Rhodesia, and South Africa, has been the main prop of Tshombe and his vicious mercenaries. They call America a "neo-colonialist power" and speak darkly of the possibility that our policies will force East Africa, reluctantly, into the Sino-Soviet camp. (2) They feel America is underwriting apartheid in South Africa by encouraging American loans and investments there. I was shown a pamphlet issued a year or two ago by the Department of Commerce and sent to businessmen and bankers all over the country recommending South Africa as a grand opportunity for profit. (3) There is particularly acute opposition to America's support of Portuguese policies in Mozambique, Angola, and Portuguese Guinea. The East African countries I visited are filled with freedom fighters from these areas who insist that the Portuguese colonial regime could not resist independence without American military and economic aid. American arms, they said over and again, are being used to kill Mozambiquans and Angolans.

I offered the answer usually given to these charges: that anyone can buy weapons made in the United States on the open market, and that the United States has an agreement with Portugal, as a NATO power, that none of the arms given her will be used outside of Portugal. The Mozambiquans and Angolans and Portuguese Guineans laughed uproariously. "Granted," they said, "that Portugal will live up to any such agreement, it remains true that Portugal has a huge store of arms which they got from the United States through NATO prior to the effective date of this agreement. So when they receive new arms from the U.S. after the agreement, they merely release the old arms they already have for use in Mozambique and Angola."

The American-Belgian airdrop into the Congo caused extreme consternation throughout East Africa. Ostensibly the airdrop was an effort to rescue a thousand "white hostages" from rebel violence, but Africans wonder whether the black hostages who were being held and killed weren't worth rescuing as well. They charge, further, that ten thousand Congolese were killed in the airdrop operation. Ten thousand lives lost to save a thousand. How many Congolese lives equal one white life? Many Africans read passages to me from a document alleged to be the diary of one of the parachutists.

After returning from Africa I encountered these passages again while reading the text of a speech delivered by the Honorable Oscar Kambona, Minister of Foreign Affairs, before the United Nations Security Council:

When we came in sight of the town from a hilltop it seemed a fine place with many modern homes and white business buildings shimmering in the evening heat haze astride the wide Lualaba River. We had heard that all Europeans had been carried off across the river by the rebels and that most of the African women and children had run away into the bush. But obviously there were people down there so, as usual, we opened up at once with everything we had. Rifles, machine guns, rocket launchers—the lot. As we thundered into the town there was a wild scram-

ble by the Africans to get from our side of the river to
the other side. Few made it. Scores were mown down as
we approached. And then we were in amongst them. They
didn't put up any fight. We just killed until, by the time
it was dark, we thought there was not one person left alive.
As we tried to settle down for the night by the river bank
we stumbled and tripped over the bodies. Some of us, tired
out, lay down to sleep right alongside corpses.

So, Africans asked me, what about the African lives? Are
they worthless?

The Congolese also charged that negotiations with the
rebels were in progress in Nairobi and making headway at
the time the airdrop was made. The decision to make the
parachute drop was taken by Foreign Minister Paul-Henri
Spaak of Belgium with the United States tagging along,
they said, and if there had been no airdrop there would
have been much less loss of life on both sides.

"Why has the U.S. taken such a disastrous posture in the
Congo?" I asked. "Obviously, economic interests." "What
do you mean, economic interests? I had no idea America
had a substantial economic interest in the Congo. The
Union Minière, the big copper combine, is largely Belgian,
maybe with some British interests." "Ah yes," they answered darkly, "but there's more control there than you
know." Some suggested that in recent months the United
States had bought a controlling interest. I could find no
evidence of this, but it was suggested. It was suggested
that we had other interests in the Congo, and some people
—not any government leaders—offered the view that the
source of our policy must be G. Mennen Williams, former
governor of Michigan and for a while a roving ambassador
to Africa. I asked why. "Because he's interested in seeing

to it that Mennen products are sold in Africa." While the case against Williams is patently absurd it is still true that American products are sold all over Africa, and the notion among Africans that we treat them as potential customers rather than as brothers has considerable plausibility to them.

I wrote a note to myself, summing up some of my feelings as I left Africa, which I think remains a valid statement of our prospects there:

> The cold war is an academic issue as far as African countries are concerned. They say, we are not about to become tools of any new imperialism from China or Russia or the United States, after having fought against political domination, colonial domination for years, and won. But if the United States remains allied with their enemies, the colonial forces, they will seek support wherever they can, and this can only mean China and Russia. I think our present policies in Africa, vis-à-vis the Congo, South Africa, and the Portuguese territories, are pushing East Africa into the arms of Peking and the Soviets. I am not convinced that we cannot avert this, that we cannot realistically alter our policies in time.

Opinions about America are milder in West Africa, though not substantially different, except of course in parts of the Congo where we are popular. This is due partly to our aid program. Nigeria, for example, has a tremendous aid program from the United States; Tanzania has not. But a sounder explanation is simple geography. East African countries are closer to South Africa and the Portuguese territories and Southern Rhodesia; they feel the pressure from these old-order nations more directly. Tanzania, for example, borders on the Congo and Southern Rhodesia. Add to this the political fact that refugee freedom fighters from the remaining colonial areas are all being harbored in East Africa (the one surprising exception to this rule is the refugees from Portuguese-controlled Angola who hole up in Tshombe's Congo). The opinions of refugee freedom fighters are usually more extreme than those of rebels who are in the thick of things.

All Africans feel that Africa is lowest on the priorities list of American policy and bitterly I recognized the truth of this. I asked students, who in fifteen years will be the leaders of Africa, what they thought our scale of priorities was, and their answer was always the same. At the top, Europe and the Russians. Next, Asia and China. Then, Latin America and Cuba. At the bottom, Africa. Indeed they felt, and again I saw the truth of what they said, that African policy was totally designed to serve America's other foreign interests. Better that we please Portugal than Africa. I was reminded of the bitterness Negroes feel when some public official says that we must improve race relations in America because racial violence is weakening our image in the world. The Negro has a stake of his own, and Africa does too.

One thing is certain. American prestige in Africa is gravely endangered by racism at home. Our segregation and discrimination are widely known in Africa and many Africans who have visited this country have been stung by it. Whenever there is an incident of racial discrimination or brutality in America it is headline news in Africa and is broadcast by radio and television all over the continent. We too bleed, Africans told me, when Negroes are bitten by dogs, and we ache when the children are beaten with billy clubs and bull whips.

Like most people outside this country, Africans do not make the fine distinctions Americans make. The federal-state distinction, for example, is a complete mystery to them. How can things happen in Mississippi or Alabama which are contrary to federal policy? they asked. The government must be hypocritical. "Why not an airdrop into Alabama?" said one student. When there is lynching in Mississippi, African headlines do not say, LYNCHING IN MISSISSIPPI; they say, LYNCHING IN U.S. After elucidating the fine points of the federal system all over Africa, I again decided that the Africans have a point.

Frequently I was asked, "What is the difference between discrimination in the United States and discrimination in South Africa?" "Well, the distinction is, of course," I said, "that in the United States segregation and discrimination are not official policies of the government. Discrimination, in most instances, is a defiance of the government. In South Africa the apartheid policy is the official policy of the government, and thus it becomes monolithic." They were not particularly impressed by the argument, but then most of the people I know in Mississippi aren't impressed by it either.

I do not wish to suggest that Africans know America better than do white Americans. They often guess wrong and betray the weaknesses of their theory. Many were convinced by Malcolm X, who traveled through Africa during the 1964 election campaign, that Johnson, a Southerner, was a racist, that Goldwater was an extreme racist, and that on a rule perhaps that doctrinal purity is always rewarded, Goldwater was bound to be elected. Many Africans were flabbergasted when Johnson won. And they must be puzzled further each time Johnson adds to his positive record in civil rights.

There is one basis for hope: throughout Africa people indicated that they believed America's unfortunate policies were of very recent vintage. Indeed, during my trip six years ago I encountered nothing like the hostility to America I encountered this time. Then I heard of America's revolutionary tradition, of how we had fought a revolution against the same empires that they now struggled against. And we were, of course, a land of twenty-two million Africans. Ironically, Africans knew far less about the sorry condition of American Negroes six years ago when conditions were worse than they know today after some progress has been made. We were also in a good position then, because we were not considered European. It had been the Europeans who dominated them. It is only recently that we have been lumped with the Europeans and that colonialist and neo-colonialist have become one. But precisely because our bad reputation is so recent, it may not be so deep. We may be able to recover our revolutionary reputation, though we will not if we do not change. It was in this connection that I perceived the unbreakable connection between America's foreign and domestic policies. The nation which in good faith can undo slavery at home must not support enslavement abroad.

I I I

As in our own civil rights revolution, the future of the new African nations will depend upon the quality of leadership they produce. I was eager to meet the new leaders and take their measure. I wanted too to study them simply as models of black men in power. Young American Negroes who aspire to political prominence do not have many native American examples to model themselves after, and statesmen, and scoundrels too, from Africa will inevitably become influential in American culture by virtue of the model they set for our youngsters. This process, in fact, has already begun. Without exception the heads and near heads of state with whom I spoke in Africa feel a special kinship with Afro-Americans and look to them to champion their cause and interpret their tribulations to other Americans.

I spoke with President Julius Nyerere of Tanzania, a new revolutionary state comprising Tanganyika (on the eastern coast of Central Africa below Kenya, above Mozambique) and the small Indian Ocean island kingdom of Zanzibar, just off the coast. Nyerere is highly cultivated and articulate, very sensitive and warm. I had the feeling, as I talked with him, that it would be a miracle if a man of such delicacy and finesse could survive in the rough-and-tumble of power politics. But he is terribly impressive. The vice-presidents, Karume and Kawawa, who survived the thicket of trade-union politics there, seem thicker skinned.

Jomo Kenyatta is, of course, a man of great charisma and almost electric appeal. I saw him speaking to a huge assemblage during his periodic visit to an outlying district about thirty miles from Nairobi. The people showered him with gifts: wood carvings, ivory figures, live chickens, sheep, goats, a bull. And when "the Old Man," as he is called, speaks, it is in a folksy fashion. He is eloquent yet jovial, and he speaks not as a fanatic but as one of them, as a father. I found him shrewd and very knowledgeable.

Haile Selassie surprised me. I had not expected such directness or political sophistication. He did not seem awed by the pomp and splendor with which he surrounds himself. He called us just a half hour before he wished to see us, and I had to drop what I was doing and dash over to the palace. I walked in and was greeted by a number of

functionaries who told me they would let me know
when HIM (His Imperial Majesty) was ready. I knew he
was to be addressed as "Your Imperial Majesty," but I'd
forgotten to ask anybody how you walk into his presence.
Do you fall on your face, do you wriggle on your stomach, do you bow three times or five times, or what? I decided to walk up to him and shake hands. When I began to
manufacture protocol, thanking him for his graciousness
and kindness in granting the audience, he smiled faintly and
waved my words aside. As the men in Harlem say, "Let's
get down to the nitty-gritty." He didn't use those words,
but I liked his manner and felt at ease immediately.

He talked freely in Amharic, the language of Ethiopia.
The interpreter he had provided us when we came to
his country did the translating. He recalled his 1954 and
1961 visits to America. On his second visit, he said, he had
asked to go to Harlem in an open car to greet the people,
but they, meaning our government, had not permitted it.
He regrets this very much. I pointed out that he would
have been perfectly safe in Harlem, and his response was,
"I was not referring to my safety, or lack of safety; I was
referring to my desire to meet the people, and your government would not allow me to meet the people face to
face." I told him that CORE could see to it that he met people if he decided to come to America again.

The Emperor is very eager to bring American Negroes
to Africa as teachers, social workers, nurses, doctors, engineers, technicians—on a contract basis. The Haile Selassie Foundation, he said, would provide financial assistance.
I told him I would pursue the idea when I returned to the
United States. I asked him if he would give me a statement
for American Negroes, Americans of African descent. He
said, "Yes, of course. Shall I give it to you verbally, or do

you want me to write it?" I said I would be grateful if he would write it. "Very well, I will, and I'll get it to you before you leave." And he did. He gave me a statement, one of the rare statements he has issued, expressing solidarity with the struggle of Americans of African descent for equality in this country; he signed it in Amharic.

The following day, as we were riding in the car which he had loaned us, we passed by his stables, which were in front of our hotel. I recognized his limousine—he comes over frequently to inspect his beautiful riding and jumping horses and feed them lumps of sugar—so I told the driver to stop. I got out and walked over to him, bowing slightly. He rolled down the window of the limousine, extended his hand, and spoke to me in perfect English. "Mr. Farmer," he said, "I want to tell the American Negroes that they have two homes: America is their home and Ethiopia is their home. They must come here any time; the whole country is theirs, because they are ours, and we are theirs."

Moving on to Nigeria, I met the man whom I had admired at a distance for many years: Nnamde Azikiwe. Like Nkrumah of Ghana, he was in America for many years as a student. When I saw him he was in the midst of the most heartbreaking political difficulties. Nigeria is a country torn in three, and time and again Azikiwe has patched the torn fabric of his nation, seemingly with tape and spit and chewing gum. If there is a man in Nigeria who has the capacity to unite the country, it is he. He has enormous popularity with the people, less with the politicians, who fear him. Wherever he goes in Nigeria, crowds gather. I don't know how they find out where he is going; perhaps it is bush telegraph. Azikiwe's coming! They engulf his car. And when he steps out in his beautiful white gown, the *akbada,* with his black skin and his hat slightly tilted on his head, it is stirring. "Ze-e-ek," they say mildly, not screaming or shouting. It is simply fantastic.

Despite the political turmoil he was enduring, he spoke to me in a relaxed manner, on a wide range of subjects. He is engrossed by all sorts of things that are happening in this country. He told me how his experience in the United States had influenced his thinking and inspired him to fight for freedom for Nigeria, even as American tradition had inspired Negroes to fight for freedom. And when he wrote the message I requested of him, he generously added this sentence: "Nigeria and CORE are co-partners in this world-wide struggle for freedom and the symbol of solidarity and unity."

Zambia's Kenneth Kaunda seemed similar to Nyerere of Tanzania—gentle, complex, an unlikely politician. But his right-hand man, Foreign Minister Kapwepke, seems tough enough for the two of them. They complement each other beautifully, and are old and fast friends. Kapwepke was quite frank about his role: "The President and I are close friends, but whenever anyone has to throw the money-changers out of the temple, or anyone else out of anywhere, the task falls in my hands." This is a brilliant team, and if anyone can solve the problems of a landlocked country bordered on two sides by hostile states, they can. Kaunda is a student of the philosophy of non-violence, and seems to practice it as much as any head of state (or serious rebel) can. We shared thoughts on the subject. He told me of the sadness he felt when he reviewed troops or otherwise surveyed the instruments of violence necessary to the modern state, and I confessed that I too was saddened by the inevitable breaches of principled non-violence in our Movement.

. . .

Moise Tshombe, the Prime Minister of the Congo, was the first person I met in that country. My plane was late, so that I did not arrive until 6:30 P.M.; Tshombe was scheduled to depart for Brussels at 10. Nonetheless, he sent word that he still wanted to see me. He came to see me at about 8:15 and remained for two full hours, delaying his flight. I found him very charming, very clever, more urbane and sophisticated than I had expected him or any Congolese person to be at the present stage of history. He is not university-educated, but he is a shrewd and apparently wealthy businessman. He breezed into the house where I was staying with his arm outstretched: *"Parlez-vous français?"* he asked, and roared with laughter when I answered, *"Un peu, un petit peu."* But I assured him that I had an interpreter.

"Oui, oui, c'est bon," he said and sat down. "I know you've heard terrible stories about the awful Tshombe and the terrible Congo and how I'm so unpopular that everyone wants to kill me, yet I must point out to you that I walk through the streets and come into this house alone, unaccompanied by any armed guard. This shows how unpopular I am, how afraid for my life."

I nodded appreciatively, and then we began talking in earnest. I asked him first why he had brought in mercenaries. All over East Africa I had found this issue of the mercenaries to be a major source of irritation. It seemed to the other African countries, as it seemed to me, that bringing in mercenaries from South Africa or Southern Rhodesia was rather like the City of New York bringing in people from Mississippi to quell a disturbance in Harlem. How could it succeed, militarily or politically?

Tshombe's response was that he had tried to get the

OAU* to intervene, but that they had rejected his plea by
one vote, leaving him with no alternative.

"I had to go some place," he said. "I had to get help.
The ANC, the National Army of the Congo, was worthless and could not fight against the rebels successfully. I
asked everybody to help: nobody came through. I asked
the United States for assistance: they gave me trucks. I
asked Belgium for help: they provided me with matériel. I
asked the OAU and they offered me their good offices. I
needed fighting men, I needed troops. Where could I get
them? The only men I could get were soldiers from South
Africa, Portugal, Rhodesia, Belgium, and I had to pay
them. I am paying them—they kept peace, they kept order.
I don't like the necessity of their being there any more than
you or anyone else."

I asked him about the possibility of negotiation with
the rebels. "Negotiate with Gbenye!" he said and talked
for fifteen minutes about the terrible atrocities committed
by the rebels under Christophe Gbenye—how they had
murdered not only whites and missionaries but also innocent Congolese, and chopped off their legs and arms, and,
in the grip of superstition, ate their hearts and livers; how
Gbenye had wiped out whole families of Congolese. I in-
terrupted to say that indeed there had been horrible crimes,
terrible atrocities on all sides. But at some time, if the
war is to come to an end, the parties must sit down and
talk.

"If Gbenye came to Léopoldville now," he said, "he
would be torn limb from limb by the relatives of the fam-

* Organization for African Unity; an organization now numbering
thirty-six African nations which was formed in 1963, in high hopes of
becoming a forum for discussion among African nations in matters of
continental interest, and when the necessary votes were achieved, a medi-
ator, even policeman, for African affairs.

ilies that he has slaughtered in Stanleyville and elsewhere. There is no army in the Congo that could guarantee his safety."

I suggested that meetings could be held elsewhere, even outside the Congo. Nairobi, I was sure, would offer its good offices for such a purpose. He smiled. His mind was open, he said, on the entire question of negotiations.

We chatted about a number of other matters concerning the Congo. He said there would be a free election. When I asked what could be done to unite Africa, he said, "Africa should unite with us. Why do the East Africans hate me and hate my government when I'm trying to unite the Congo?" I reminded him that the freedom fighters in Mozambique, Southern Rhodesia, South Africa, and Southwest Africa charge his regime with being antagonistic to their interests and aspirations and with giving support to the colonial powers.

"But we provide sanctuary for the freedom fighters and the refugees from Angola. Their headquarters are right here. We provide them with refuge and they train their troops here. They make forays into Angola, and when the Portuguese push them back, they can run back across the border to safety. So we are supporting the freedom fighters." Thus he defended himself. Yet I found to my own satisfaction in Africa that Tshombe is hated by the East African countries for good and sufficient reasons. While still a local leader in Katanga, it is alleged he financed and supported the opposition to Jomo Kenyatta in Kenya, before Kenya became independent; the opposition to Nyerere in Tanzania, before Tanzania became independent; the opposition to Kaunda in Zambia, and probably also that to Obote in Uganda. For want of a better interpretation of his actions, this must be interpreted as supporting colonialism. Understandably, the leaders of these countries fear that if he turned against them once, before they became heads of state, he will try to do it again. In the light of their feelings I see no possibility that the East African countries will consent to work with Tshombe, or to accept him as a partner. Tshombe reminded me most of some presidents I have known of Southern Negro colleges—tough, skillful, with the balance of a gyroscope. Like them, I thought, Tshombe knows how to keep black folk in their place.

Joseph Kasavubu, President of the Congo, is a totally different personality. I was impressed with his shrewdness; not quick and flashy sophistication, but a more philosophical, thoughtful type of intelligence. Perhaps it was because of his slightly Oriental countenance that he impressed me as a contemplative man. He is of Chinese ancestry, dating back to the time when Chinese were taken to the Congo by the thousands to build a railroad. He was younger than I had expected and very relaxed, talking at great length in answer to my questions. I would ask him a question and he would lean back and think for a while, like an Oriental philosopher, narrowing his eyes and chuckling to himself as if contemplating his answer and being amused by its implications. Then he would begin to talk. He would circle the question, move in on it, back away from it, circle it again. But in the final analysis, his answers were not evasions; they were his way of acknowledging the complexities of the issues under discussion.

"Negotiate with the rebels? Well, Mr. Farmer, negotiation means many things to many people. What do we mean by negotiation? What are negotiations and what sort of context are they to be held in? Now, sometimes there are talks between one sovereign nation and another sovereign nation—that's a negotiation. The nations are equals. Sometimes there are talks between forces within a nation—that too is called negotiation. But if there are talks within a nation, it has to be very clearly decided whether the parties are people of equal status, equal authority, equal importance. And we have to determine what the context of the talks will be—there must be some framework. Usually when talks are held within a nation, they are called negotiations and the framework for those talks is the law, the law of the land. Then are we suggesting that there be talks with the rebels in which the context or the framework will be the Congo law? Are we suggesting, too, that the rebels will come in as an equal force, to sit down across the table and negotiate with the government as equals? After all, they claim to be the government, you know, and Gbenye claims to be President, Prime Minister, or whatever it is, of the Congo. So will they negotiate as equals?"

This was a thoughtful approach to the problem of negotiations. But then he went on in a rather different vein. "I am a devout Catholic and I believe in the absolution of sins. But first there has to be a contrite heart: you have to confess, you have to humble yourself, and then your sins can be forgiven. I have forgiven many people in the past, I have commuted many prison sentences, I have pardoned many prisoners in prison, political prisoners and otherwise, but only after they had humbled themselves, begged forgiveness and confessed their sins. So, the rebels? Are they willing to confess their sins and promise to go and sin no more?"

Kasavubu clearly is a man of depth. But the long-range hope of the Congo lies in the university students presently being trained for leadership. Their unanimous opinion was that the Congo must get rid of both the rebels and the Tshombe government. Both sides, the students felt, have been so involved in chicanery and corruption and brutality that they have lost any possibility of uniting the country or of stabilizing it or even of governing it. A new third force is needed, perhaps some of the trade-union leaders, Bo-Boliko and others.

The morning before I left the Congo, two officials of Patrice Lumumba's old party came to talk with me. It was quite curious. Each one called independently of the other and asked to see me. Both had been trying unsuccessfully to get in touch with me all the previous day. They called in the morning and we set up appointments half an hour apart. They came in different entrances and we put them in different rooms, hoping that neither one would know that the other was there.

The first one came in and identified himself and spoke quite eloquently about the fact that he bore a resemblance to Lumumba whose martyred memory inspires rebels all over Africa: he was tall and thin and wore his hair like Lumumba and had a goatee. He said that Gbenye's rebels had betrayed the revolution, had betrayed Lumumba and everything he had stood for. Lumumba was a great man who preached non-violence, but the rebels were the most violent and bloodthirsty of folk. Lumumba preached anti-tribalism, but the rebels were preaching tribalism and manipulating tribal loyalties to serve their own selfish purposes. If Lumumba were alive, he would be driven to say, "Thank God I'm not a Lumumbist!"

"Tshombe and the Tshombe government," he went on, in essentially the same vein as the university students, "are as bad or worse. They too have slaughtered hundreds of thousands. Tshombe has betrayed not the revolution but the Congo, and there is no hope for him. There must be a middle force, a moderate group. The rebels now are in the camp of the Communists. Tshombe is in the camp of the reactionaries and the colonialists. We must have a middle force that is in nobody's camp."

I asked him how much support he had. He insisted that 80 to 90 per cent of the Congolese would support his party, the Lumumbist party.

"Then you will win the election," I said.

"No, the election will not, cannot, be free, because most of the leaders who would be campaigning for office have been jailed by Tshombe and cannot campaign. Furthermore, our party has no funds. We can't campaign. We can't send anybody around the country. We can't even send anybody to Stanleyville, we don't have transportation money, so we can't win the election. The election will be a fraud and we know it. What you should do, Brother Farmer, is go back to the United States and persuade Johnson and your government to give us the backing that we need, and then we can unite the Congo."

The other leader, the secretary-general of the party, who was in the other room, heard his colleague's voice as he was leaving and whispered to me, "Watch out for this fellow. He's only talking for himself, you know, pushing himself." The first gentleman then poked his head back in: "Oh, by the way, when you get to the States, can you finance a trip to America for me and one or two of my friends, to interpret the Congo to your country?"

I found Nkrumah the most difficult person to see in Africa. I was in Ghana for three days. Although my request to meet with Nkrumah was put in as soon as I arrived, I received no response at all until the morning of the last day. Then *Osagyefo* ("Savior"), as he is called, arranged to see me at 12:30. Evidently he was waiting to see the reports from his secret service, to be sure that I was not representing the CIA or the State Department. Once he understood that I was taking an independent line, he agreed to see me.

The precautions taken for his life are great. In the huge grounds surrounding the Flagstaff House, we had to go through any number of guard checks at which I had to prove repeatedly that I was indeed James Farmer. At length the guards pointed me up to the palace, and after a few minutes *Osagyefo* was ready. We had to go through three locked doors with neither knobs nor handles which swung open electrically when the guard pressed an invisible button.

I finally walked through the swinging doors into Nkrumah's large office, and he came striding forward to shake hands. He was a smaller man than I had anticipated, but with an unexpected magnetism. He does, of course, inspire loyalty in a certain number of people. I thought I could also see in his face the ruthlessness which has destroyed many of his former friends, now exiled or in detention. He is a hard and tough but essentially intelligent man who, I think, is able to separate the personal from the political. He knew I disagree with him politically; I implied it without making any direct statements. He merely shrugged his shoulders. He mentioned then the great American Negro thinker, W. E. B. Du Bois, to whom he had given a home at the end of his days. Du Bois finally took out citizenship in Ghana and died there at the age of ninety-six.

I told him I disagreed very strongly with Du Bois, politically, but that I was outraged by the attempts of some people in my country to erase his greatness. Nkrumah agreed and said that this was one of the reasons he had offered the old man a home and something constructive to do. And he agreed with me that Du Bois probably died happy. He thought it was a great thing for Ghana to have taken him in as it did. "Of course," he said, "you disagree with him politically and I didn't agree with him on everything politically, but personal matters have very little to do with the political. For example, the United States ambassador here and I are personal friends. I visit him in his home, he visits me in my home; we get together very frequently although we don't agree politically. I know that he is the ambassador of his country and has to represent, express, and defend the official views and the policy of his country. And he does it, he does it admirably. I have different views. But this does not affect our personal friendship." Nkrumah does not seem to apply these sentiments to those who may be a political threat to him, but what politician does? I think he is in real danger of assassination, because he obviously does have enemies. Anyone who seeks to maintain his power and leadership through hard-fist methods must live a precarious existence.

But on the positive side, nowhere in Africa did I find such energy, such a sense of motion and direction. They are nationalizing some things, of course, but they are creating their country, not just talking about it. Buildings are shooting up all over the place. They are starting theater groups, art groups, writers' groups, developing educational television. They recognize that most of the people are unable to afford television sets at the usual prices, so they are preparing to go into partnership with a Japanese company to manufacture television sets cheaply and then sell them at low cost to the people. In the outlying districts they plan to put up public television sets so that the public can come and view at no cost the plays, news, and educational programs that the government will present.

Nkrumah seems to have a hand in everything. Everything crosses his desk for his approval, and apparently he
studies each item and approves or disapproves it. There is
something mightily impressive about this little man who
sits at his desk in daily fear for his own life, yet virtually
controls the heartbeat of the country. I told him how impressed I was by his energy and motion.

Nkrumah's attitudes and the enforced attitudes of his
state are as extreme as any in East Africa. But he is not
completely trusted there or anywhere. He apparently has
his finger in affairs all over the continent. It is said that he
undermined the proposed East African Federation. It is
well known, of course, that he dreams of leading a
United Africa, though others, such as Egypt's Nasser,
dream similarly. I felt it most unlikely that there could be
unification between peoples from the Sahara and the
sub-Sahara regions, so different culturally. Indeed I de-
tected little motion toward unity of any sort. Most of the
leaders, at this stage, are struggling first to form nations
from the tribes that exist within their borders. The idea of
"a nation" is abstract enough to most tribe members—a
"united Africa" is even more remote to them. There may
be forms of economic unification, but political unification
seems implausible for now.

In general I found the top-ranking officials in the
African nations men of the highest caliber, and there
were obviously many brilliant prospects in the universities. But beneath the highest echelon, ability seems to
drop precipitously, a remainder, clearly, of shortsighted
colonial policy. For the moment the simple paucity of able
personnel seems to inhibit the development of democratic
governments as do the simple economic requirements of
rapidly modernizing and industrializing sorely underde-

veloped nations. Our own imperfect republic will be ill-advised to expect perfect republics, or even models of capitalism, from these emerging nations.

I V

I had not imagined how poorly our communications media inform us about Africa.

Distortions in our press do us inestimable damage in Africa, where the American press is perused minutely. *Time* magazine's piece on Tanzania is a case in point: typical *Time* reporting, snide, cute, clever, and thoroughly inaccurate. Imagine! "Nothing could be zanier than Tanzania." Nyerere was very distressed about the piece, and I can't blame him.

Very little has been reported about the atrocities and crimes committed in the Congo by the mercenaries and their friends, the government troops. After seeing the situation, there can be no doubt that the rebels have committed unspeakable crimes, but atrocity for atrocity, the mercenaries equal the rebels, and in one sense surpass them, for they are trespassers and this compounds any crime they commit.

Newspapermen, as a *New York Times* correspondent pointed out, are denied entrance to Stanleyville unless they agree not to write about the mercenaries. Congolese I spoke to in Stanleyville begged me not to besmirch the good name of visiting troops.

From personal experience I know that Americans are transporting mercenaries, and this too is not widely known. I traveled in a U. S. Air Corps transport, an enormous machine, whose rear end opened up wide enough to permit a truck to be driven in. I was sitting in the cockpit with the pilot, the co-pilot, the navigator, and three airmen; they all had pistols. And in the back I found mercenaries being transported from Léopoldville to Stanleyville. A sleazy bunch, every one with a pistol on his hip.

I have seen this breed in our own Southland. They were on a "nigger-killing" expedition. Most of them were people who fled to Rhodesia or South Africa at the time of the Mau Mau in Kenya, or fled from the Central Africa Federation or Nyasaland at the time of independence. Some of them, the Congolese told me, brought their own acetylene torches; they were going to make a killing, not only of Congolese, but of money. They broke into banks, opened vaults, broke plate-glass windows, pillaged stores, cleaned out cash registers and safes, and pocketed the money, all the time killing Congolese at will. This story simply has not been told. *And these men could not have operated without the support we gave them.*

All the Congolese in Stanleyville had white handkerchiefs on their heads, meaning, "I am a friendly Congolese, don't shoot me, Mr. Mercenary." And some people advised me to put a handkerchief on my head, for safety's sake. But I've had enough of handkerchief-heads and declined.

v

What can America do?

I think it is clear that our policies in Africa must be changed and changed soon, though of course there is a limit to what we can do, since events and trends in Africa as elsewhere are largely beyond our control.

Let us consider the three main sources of trouble in Africa, in inverse order of difficulty: the Portuguese territories, South Africa, and the Congo.

As for Portugal, my feeling is that we should tell the Portuguese government that as a country with a revolutionary heritage, the United States cannot be placed in the position of even indirectly supporting any continuation of colonialism. Without going so far as to join in the fighting against the Portuguese in Mozambique and Angola, we should absolutely refuse to assist, with arms or funds, Portugal's attempts to maintain colonialism in her African possessions. By taking a firm line, we might jeopardize our base in the Azores, but a number of our diplomats and military men with whom I've spoken do not believe that the Azores are any longer a military necessity to the United States. And even if they are, our relationship with Black Africa, which is also at stake, is more crucial.

To South Africa, I think, we should apply economic sanctions. Not that they would be likely to cause the collapse of the South African economy, but in Africa the moral effect of such a step would be enormous. The important point is to take a definite position in support of the aspirations of the African liberation movement and in definite opposition to the South African government.

The idea of economic sanctions is now firmly part of the civil rights armory, and after the passage of the Civil Rights Act of 1964, particularly, Title VI, which authorizes the federal government to withhold funds from all programs and projects which practice or condone segregation, it is part of the federal armory as well. A fully enforced economic boycott, mounted by the government in conjunction with labor, business, and consumer, would bring Mississippi to heel in six months. If a similar line were applied to South Africa it might achieve excellent results. In addition to withholding its own funds from South Africa our government should urge private industry and banking and financial institutions not to invest in South Africa. It is often objected that this is a free-enterprise country and the government cannot tell businessmen what to do with their money. But, in fact, governmental policy already affects American investments abroad: certainly businessmen are not free to invest in the Soviet Union or Red China or Cuba. For our part, in our usual persuasive fashion, CORE will try to convince individual firms to desist from helping enslave our brothers in Africa with ill-considered investments.

As for the Congo, there are obviously no panaceas. I will start by saying what should not be our approach. When I was in East Africa, many of the younger East Africans told me we should get out of the Congo altogether. I told them I thought this nonsense. No major power would withdraw from so important a place as the Congo. It is both implausible and undesirable, as every one of the African nations which are nudging Congo affairs along knows. The question is, Can we be in the Congo without being on the side of either the rebels or the Tshombe government, both of which I feel are unacceptable?

There are certain tasks to which American diplomacy could profitably be directed. Somehow a permanent cease-fire and disengagement must be arranged. When I talked to Tshombe and Kasavubu in Léopoldville, I asked them whether they would accept negotiations through the OAU. Neither of them explicitly rejected the idea. Their principal objections were first that the participating nations in the OAU are themselves interested parties and therefore unlikely arbiters; secondly, they said that Gbenye, the alleged rebel leader, could not speak for the rebels, and if he arranged an unsuitable compromise, he would be dumped. In answering, I held that there were some neutrals among the OAU nations—I mentioned Nigeria, Ethiopia, Senegal, Dahomey—and said their good offices and perhaps peacekeeping troops might be used. As for the argument that Gbenye was not representative of the rebels, I said it was purely theoretical. If the rebels repudiated an agreement made by Gbenye, after negotiations had been laboriously arranged, the effect would be to so discredit the rebels and so cut off their support as to destroy them. So I feel the United States should join with other nations in urging a settlement. Whether these efforts should be initiated through the UN or the OAU or through impromptu diplomatic channels, I cannot say.

Following the cease-fire, there must be negotiations between the government and the rebels, and the mercenaries must be kept out, perhaps by OAU troops. It is clear that there can be no solution as long as the mercenaries are near; their presence is an outrage.

This much is clear to me. I see no solution in letting Tshombe force the rebels out of the Congo into the Sudan or in letting him exterminate the rebels. The reasons for rebellion would remain and rebels would appear again and again. It goes without saying, of course, that nothing will be "solved" until the economic needs of the Congo are met through better educational facilities and greater prosperity. The hope of the Congo lies in a third force: perhaps it is lying dormant among the brilliant university students—the politicians, administrators, and professional classes of tomorrow. All of those I spoke to felt it imperative to get rid of the present factions and end the chicanery, corruption, crime, and brutality. Perhaps some trade-union figure like Bo-Boliko, the head of a large Christian trade-union group, is the answer.

A change of policy in Washington is not enough by itself to change our image in Africa unless it is dramatically implemented. I believe it would be a wise move to summon our ambassadors in Africa to a conference to review our entire African policy and learn their ideas about possible changes. The American officials I met in Africa struck me favorably, with a few specific exceptions. Many of them disagree with present American policy. As one official put it to me, "We don't want to become extinct on this continent, but the way we're moving now, we will be." The very act of calling the ambassadors together would have considerable impact on Africa and if we could announce a major change in policy soon after, we would stir approval in many African hearts. I might reiterate here Nyerere's suggestion that Humphrey go to Africa.

Then there is the question of Negro representation on our diplomatic staff and the American Negro presence in Africa in general. There is a hoary old saw which says that Africans don't want American Negroes in Africa. Nothing could be further from the truth. Africans asked me again and again why there are not more Americans of African descent attached to the American Embassy (there is usually one Negro official in an embassy, *the* Negro). Why, they asked, are there not more in the Peace Corps and other government programs? As I have mentioned, Haile Selassie offered to help pay for Negro technical and professional assistance, and I heard a similar offer in Zambia. Naturally the United States government cannot do this alone; there must be some initiatives from the Negro community and private agencies and organizations. But some government initiative would be helpful.

Finally, I think there should be a wide variety of programs to encourage contact and cultural exchange between American Negroes and Africans. Exchanges of artists, dance groups, musicians, writers, under private and federal auspices. I think other civil rights leaders should visit Africa, if possible for longer than I did. Civil rights leaders should seek conferences with the President and the Secretary of State, and attempt to influence policy. After my five-week trip I stated to U.S. government officials many of the thoughts I have gathered here. And there must be a grass-roots effort. CORE should create an interest in African affairs in its chapters, sponsoring lectures and cultural programs.

Africa has entered the community of nations even as the Negro has entered the community of Americans. Whenever newcomers enter any community, the oldtimers must move over and make room, undo some selfish habits, and learn the habit of listening to their new neighbors. Of course, the newcomers also must listen considerately. If the American Negro can help America listen better to Africa, and Africa listen better to America; if he can help bring American foreign policy abreast of the other black revolutions in this world, he will have performed well his duty as citizen.

VI

I am convinced the nonaligned African nations want to be on good terms with America. But nonalignment works only if East and West can meet as equals. If one side becomes an enemy, then nonalignment is dropped, and out of defense and the desire for survival new alliances are forged. I cannot argue too strongly that the present posture of America in Africa is driving many nonaligned nations toward the East. Africa inevitably will become a force in world affairs. This is a huge continent with untold wealth, much of which is only now being discovered. In Nigeria and the Congo they are discovering oil every week; there are great deposits of diamonds and copper. For every possible reason—moral, political, economic—we cannot afford to alienate this land.

I confess to some self-interest in the matter, indeed very immediate self-interest. If Africa turns to the Chinese, inevitably the black nationalist organizations in America will ally with groups like the Maoist Progressive Labor Movement (PLM). PLM has constantly tried to forge an alignment between itself and the nationalists, even as the Chinese are supporting revolutionary nationalism in Africa. During the 1964 Harlem riots nationalist groups joined CORE and other civil rights organizations in passing a resolution rejecting a PLM proposal to march again into Harlem. "We do not favor any black man dying in order to help the Chinese Communists."

But this could change. If East Africans turn more and more to the Chinese, so will American black nationalists turn to PLM and their like. Such an alliance would pose a really serious, almost terrifying problem for civil rights organizations and for the country as a whole. Let us hope that this will never come about. It need not, if American policy in Africa is meaningfully redirected. But time is running out.

7

FREEDOM—WHEN?

O N E measure of how much the civil rights movement has achieved in the decade since the school desegregation decision of the Supreme Court is that we are now beginning to think and plan "beyond civil rights." If we need to designate a turning point, we might mention the March on Washington in the summer of 1963 which, too few people noticed, was not only for "freedom" but for "jobs" as well. Until then we understood the race problem as a problem of discrimination and segregation. If only the nation would lift the unnatural barriers to economic, social, and political opportunity for Negroes, we thought; if only Negroes had full protection and equal privileges and immunities, in law and social fact, our task would be complete.

Today, when much, though by no means all, of the civil rights legislation we have worked for is on the books, we are beginning to realize that civil rights alone may not be enough. Freedom is an art demanding practice, and too many of us are unpracticed. Some of the programs we now project—mobilizing local and national political action, voter registration and education, local community-development and self-help programs, cultural enrichment —are designed to encourage such practice. The fact that Negroes *can* vote, to put the matter most simply, does not mean that they will or that they will do justice to themselves and their interests when they do.

Then, too, we have come to understand that a blind, broken horse will not move smartly out of an open gate. Perhaps being deprived of civil rights is the explanation for the pervasive impoverishment of Negroes, and certainly the Negro will not rise from poverty until his rights are secure, but the simple fact is that he *is* poor and does suffer all the impoverishment of soul and spirit that chronic poverty implies in America. Offering him equal rights, even equal opportunity, at this late date, without giving him a special boost, is the kind of cruel joke American individualism has played on the poor throughout American history. And so CORE and the movement of which we are part plan compensatory and remedial programs to provide the necessary boost.

And "beyond" these considerations we have come to realize that Negro poverty is a special case of the general problem of poverty in America. The fact that Negroes who are one tenth of the population comprise one fourth of the nation's poor leads one to conclude not only that Negroes are uniquely victimized, but also that three quarters of the forty million or so poor in this country are white. As cybernetics and automation proceed apace the problem may become more acute. Obviously, Negro poverty will be eliminated only when all poverty is eliminated; accordingly, we are glimpsing programs and policies which

will force the nation to deal radically with this radical condition.

It is inviting to think exclusively from a perspective beyond civil rights but it is dangerous too, for we may be
seduced into forgetting the remaining workaday tasks. Already the ideologues are telling the movement that civil
rights are outmoded; that demonstrations and other forms
of direct action are a dead letter or at best a mopping-up
exercise, and that the movement must suddenly rethink all
its assumptions. To a movement made up of people who
ask constantly, What, concretely, can we do now, at
this meeting, in this particular season of our discontent?
this can be cruel and irresponsible advice. Unless, of course,
one has some specific program to offer. It is easy to dream
bold dreams, it is harder to translate them into a program.
Actually, civil rights, while no longer our exclusive concern, are not as anachronistic as the ideologues suggest,
and it seems to me wise, in this discussion of the future of
the movement, to look first at the civil rights tasks which
remain before turning to new vistas.

I. CIVIL RIGHTS

One rule of thumb Negroes have learned well, from
having their thumbs smashed so often, is that a law on the
books means nothing when it is not vigorously implemented. Many of the Northern states in which Negroes
dwell in sizeable numbers have strong fair housing, fair
employment, fair labor practices legislation; yet landlords
and realtors still contrive to keep desirable areas lily-white,
and employers and some union officials still keep Negroes
out of jobs and apprenticeship programs.

There are several things we will do about this. For one,
we can bring vigorous anti-discrimination suits under ap-

propriate state and local ordinances which have fallen into disuse—partly, we must confess, because of our own emphasis on federal action. As always, these suits will be more speedily implemented in a climate of direct action and specific protest. We will continue to persuade individuals and groups guilty of discrimination to mend their ways if not their hearts. A real estate agency guilty of illegal discrimination will suffer the inconvenience of pickets and the humiliation of public disclosure, as will a derelict landlord or employer or union. When circumstances warrant, we will organize economic boycotts. We will, of course, continue to enlist the support and co-operation of sympathetic groups in the North—while demanding that Kennedy's weak Executive Order on housing be made stronger.

Two areas in particular, fair housing and school desegregation, promise continuing struggle. The year 1964 marked an alarming regression in some states—California, Washington, and Michigan—where fair housing and open occupancy legislation was defeated or repealed. California is especially alarming. While voting heavily for Johnson in 1964, Californians not only repealed extremely progressive housing laws by referendum, but actually made it unconstitutional to pass such legislation in the future. Opinion polls documenting wide sympathy for the Negro cause among Northerners still find them adding "but not next door . . ."—and we have not seen the last attempt to undo fair housing and open occupancy legislation. Housing segregation, of course, is a key to many other ills in the North, like *de facto* school segregation; indeed one of the strongest arguments against school desegregation is that segregation in the North is the result of housing patterns rather than deliberate school policy. It is a vicious circle, of course. One of the ways to break it is to couple our fair housing demand with our drive for school desegregation, thereby exposing the hypocrisy of those who plead "Housing!" in evading desegregation of schools.

There have been regressive developments in school desegregation too. It is now clear that we will not have as much help from the courts as we had hoped. In three decisions the Supreme Court disclosed its determination, for the moment, to keep hands off Northern schools and to leave the question of racial balance to local school boards. And in a tragic amendment to Title IV of the Civil Rights Act of 1964, Congress explicitly refused to extend the school desegregation provisions of the act to cases of "de facto segregation." I firmly believe that *de facto* segregation is as unconstitutional as so-called *de jure* segregation and await the day when the Court extends the logic of the *Brown* decision to Northern segregation, but for the moment we are thrown back upon local devices and activities. We can predict an intense struggle. Whites will organize into a variety of associations "to protect the neighborhood school concept," they will say, using the techniques of demonstration, legal action, and political pressure, which we taught them. We must, in return, be shrewd and flexible. We will need to demonstrate and boycott, reconciling the public to the justice of our position. And we shall need to exert political pressure more directly than in the past* and as I shall point out in a moment, make honorable alliances, when fitting and necessary, with other groups who support our cause.

I think an important and soothing new ingredient will be added to the public stew over housing and schools as Negroes and whites come to realize that desegregation and not total integration, total assimilation, is our goal. In parallel activity with our demands that schools and neighborhoods be desegregated, we will be regenerating the

* See below.

ghetto for those who will choose to live there, and we will be emphasizing the word "quality" in our demand for "quality integrated education." A prouder, more self-reliant Negro community will emerge, and it will become clear that assimilation is not what Negroes desire.

In the South our civil rights task is, for the moment, more elemental and clear cut. Here there are still massive and flagrant denials of the most elemental rights: the right to vote, to run for office, to serve on juries; the right to equal protection of the laws; the right to free speech and unhampered political expression; the right to equal enjoyment of public facilities and accommodations. The widespread school segregation in the South is demonstrably the result of a recent history of legal segregation and therefore under the scrutiny of the Supreme Court.

Our technique in the South thus far has been to act directly upon segregated public accommodations and facilities and to prod the federal government into administering and implementing the law and into passing new laws which are needed. We have had three voting bills since 1957, and the comprehensive Civil Rights Bill of 1964 at least touched on every area of our concern in the South, though not as forthrightly or courageously as we would have liked. The Voting Rights Law of 1965 is weaker than we had desired. Its failure to act on the poll tax issue and the lack of firm protection for Negroes exercising their right to register and vote are now abundantly clear. And the implementation —with Attorney General Katzenbach appointing federal registrars to relatively few of the more than four hundred eligible counties—is far too timid.

Still, the recent history of legislation in this area at least permits us to foresee the day when Negroes in the South will vote freely, and will have equal access to public ac-

commodations and somewhat freer access to job opportunities, and will be better protected from harm and harass-
ment when they exercise their rights. But equality will not
happen simply because there are laws on the books.

Predictably, the South will use every device available to
delay the application of the law or elude its grasp. We can
expect obstructionist litigation challenging the constitu-
tionality of the new laws. And where forced the South will
move no farther than it has to, to satisfy the nation's command. Tokenism will become a science. Racist governors
—like Johnson in Mississippi and Wallace of Alabama—
are already diligently trying to project "a better image"
of their states, lulling government and citizenry into a
false sense of Southern progress. They will purr before the
television cameras on "Meet the Press" and learn how to
pronounce "Neeegro" and deluge the media with propa-
ganda about race progress in the Southland, displaying
conspicuous moderation, reminding listeners—who may
be weary of the race question on other scores—that moderation is a virtue. We can expect Southern policemen to
show more temperance—beating fewer heads and causing
smaller headlines. And as the South learns to be more cov-
ert in its villainy, it will become more and more unpleasant
for the federal government to exert its will, and we can
expect periodic flaggings of attention from our national
government. Will the government utilize its considerable
powers diligently? Will federal funds be cut off from discriminatory activities? Will the FBI make arrests and the
Justice Department prosecute to the full measure of the
law? Will the President continue to place his enormous prestige and persuasive power in the cause of right? We must
see to it that these questions are answered affirmatively.
We must exhibit Southern evasions of the law to the
naked eye with cogent demonstrations and protests. We

must register voters diligently and see to it that they are not bought off or frightened by the enormous impetus to Preserve-All in the South. We must become adept in the modes of political pressure and use our awesome voting power to the fullest.

Eventually, we will succeed in bringing the South to the point where it will face the problems the North faces now. One of the things this will mean is that civil rights in the South will become a local matter, hammered out among Southerners. We cannot expect and should not wish to have a federal presence forever, though we don't want federal attentions to end one minute before the Negro has the power to cope with the South as an equal among equals. There is a mythology which holds that the South will "solve its problems" more quickly than the North, because unlike the fractured and anguished cities of the North, Southern towns are tied in "love and community." Reconciliation, the myth runs, will be swift and dramatic. This sentiment is usually uttered by whites trying to persuade the government to cease and desist its attentions, though I have heard militant Negroes say the same thing. I doubt this strongly. As legal segregation in the South becomes *de facto* segregation, as Negroes get some money and education and the mobility these bring, as the South industrializes and new Northern-like cities emerge and the Negro moves from the land to the city, it seems to me that the South will become more and more like the North and the problems of the sections will be the same.

Northern civil rights workers will continue to exert pressure on the South. One of the techniques we shall exploit is the national economic boycott. There has been considerable discussion of Martin Luther King's calls for a boycott of Alabama and Mississippi. While national boy-

cotts are a sound idea, I feel that the buckshot method
of dealing with an entire state may be unsound, hurting
everyone in general and no one in particular. The boycotts should be more selective. Perhaps against products
of a particular factory, demonstrably discriminatory in
its hiring practices, or against bonds floated by a particular
school district which is obdurately segregationist. The purpose of the boycott is to add another dimension of pressure on the South and to help develop a national sense
of responsibility for conditions in the South. Many Northerners are incredulous when we tell them that they are responsible for segregation in the South and can do something
about it. The boycott pinpoints their responsibility and
their opportunities.*

I am often asked what would constitute a successful boycott. Many feel that the national boycotts have been a
total failure. Their definition of a success, I might say,
invokes images of a beleaguered fort, utterly surrounded
by hostile Indians who are cutting them off from food and
water. When the last living soldier staggers out, surrender-
ing the fort for a crust of bread, the boycott is deemed a
success. Nothing so dramatic will happen. But there are
subtler effects: a factory all set to move into a Southern
town thinks twice and delays its decision; interest on bonds
for a new school goes a point higher. Businessmen and the
politicians they talk to can be very sensitive to these things.
The very threat of a boycott is enough to make a busi-

---

* For the record, in the spring of 1965 the Childs Security Corporation,
a subsidiary of C. F. Childs & Co., sent a letter to Governor George C.
Wallace stating that the concern would not deal in the state's bonds.
When Wallace had announced that the State of Alabama did not have
enough money to protect the marchers from Selma to Montgomery, the
Childs people wrote, saying the state was obviously in terrible financial
shape and a poor investment risk. Also, since the time of the civil rights
murders in Philadelphia, Mississippi, in June, 1964, Baxter & Co. of New
York and Cleveland has refused to handle Mississippi and Alabama bonds.

nessman uneasy. There will be no apocalypse, but the boy-cott technique will be very useful.

In three areas in particular we shall need to spur the federal government to greater effort. First, we must spur the government to vigorous use of its most powerful weapon: the withdrawal of financial support from any dis-criminatory activity. The range of federal spending is enor-mous. Hardly a school district in the South could exist without federal help. Many school districts in the South, fearing the loss of federal assistance, have signed a pledge to desegregate; but we must see to it that they are held to the pledge. Bank deposits are federally insured, as are many home and farm loans. Road building and every man-ner of urban development receive federal assistance. Large chunks of industry in the South exist on government con-tracts or subcontracts. If the threat of economic with-drawal were made palpable, an army of Southern bigots would alter their ways.

Second, there is the area of fair employment practices. Title VII of the Civil Rights Act establishes an independent commission with power to initiate proceedings on behalf of aggrieved parties. The commission did not come into effect until July, 1965, and in the year between passage of the bill and the start of the commission's life the Admin-istration did very little to prepare itself or the South for vigorous prosecution of Title VII. Despite the appointment of a distinguished and earnest chairman, Franklin D. Roose-velt, Jr., the failure of the Administration to use effectively the year's hiatus is evident in the fact that there was not one case of an affirmative order against a discriminatory com-pany or union in the first six months of the commissioner's life. Appointments should have been made much earlier than they were and educational materials should have been printed and distributed to Southern employers telling them what the law is and what they must do. As we know, the Negro in the

South is largely impoverished. In the Black Belt states—South Carolina, northern Florida, Georgia, Alabama, Mississippi, Louisiana—75 per cent of Negroes live on annual incomes of less than $3,000. In Mississippi, 37 per cent of Negro families exist on less than $20 a week. It could very well happen that the Southern economy will expand just enough in the next ten years to uplift the millions of whites who suffer from the antiquated system, leaving the Negro as before. To prevent this, fair employment practices will be essential.

Third, we must continue to prompt the federal government to provide police protection where there is none in the South. The Justice Department and the President have been extremely reluctant to create what they call "a federal police force" for the South. But they do not say how they expect police terror and intimidation to end without policing of Southerners. In some places where Negroes vote, sheriffs, like the one elected in Plaquemine, become prudently civilized. Where local officials are doing their jobs, federal marshals and investigators need not act. But where there are police-state tactics pure and simple, then the government must move in, making arrests directly and prosecuting under strong federal laws. We will need to demonstrate and probably bleed and die some more to make the government understand this.

One final consideration in this survey of civil rights tasks: It has been widely said that when there are enough jobs and homes for everyone, there will be no civil rights problems. Discrimination, the argument runs, is a function of scarcity. And some conclude from this that we should concentrate on eliminating scarcity rather than on fighting for equal access to insufficient opportunities (how *we* can eliminate scarcity is not made clear). Realism instructs, however, that in the foreseeable future, twenty-five or thirty years, the best we can hope for is that scarcity will be alleviated. Even the most pie-eyed economists would agree that if poverty could be cut by 75 per cent in two decades, the economy would have behaved brilliantly. How many of the remaining 25 per cent will be Negroes? We should not suppose that America has suddenly become less clever in keeping the black man down. Clearly, we must guard against discrimination every step of the way to total affluence, prowling about private companies and government programs and labor unions for signs that the Negro is getting less than his complete due.

The War on Poverty is a case in point. Its conception filled with excitement, its execution drearily inadequate: $1.5 billion annually when we should be spending $30 billion. On whom, we must ask, will the predictably inadequate anti-poverty funds be spent? One economist has shrewdly observed that the anti-poverty program discriminates in favor of the "deserving poor," leaving the "undeserving poor" to their squalor. By this he means that the government will spend money only on those who are likely to be dramatically helped by the program, perhaps in order to prove to pennypinching congressmen that the program is worthwhile. But who are the "deserving poor?" More important, who will decide? We must be vigilant and be for ourselves.

The question is, Should the Negro, last hired, first fired, most impoverished and most poorly prepared of any group in America, be in the vanguard to eliminate scarcity, or should he be looking to see that he receives all he deserves of what there is? Obviously, the answer is, Both. What I have tried to suggest is that the one should not be at the expense of the other. Why is it that ideologues always ask the most dedication and idealistic sacrifice from those lowest on the ladder? We should expect realism from the needy, and a persistent emphasis on traditional civil rights, I think, is only realistic.

We shall continue, therefore, to be a civil rights movement and we will maintain the posture we have shown in recent years: demonstrations by local chapters, negotiation and picketing against discrimination, civil disobedience where necessary, public witness, direct confrontation, creative disorder, and hopefully, reconciliation. In brief, CORE will be CORE.

II. BEYOND CIVIL RIGHTS: POLITICAL PARTICIPATION

In April, 1965, sixteen New York City CORE chapters announced their opposition to the re-election of Mayor Robert F. Wagner. Many people were startled by this breach of nonpartisanship and, to be sure, the announcement did signal a new departure in CORE policy. Traditionally, civil rights organizations have been content to obtain the right to full political participation and have maintained strict neutrality in politics. The more or less open support they gave to President Johnson—or, more precisely, their open opposition to Goldwater—was an exception proving the rule. We seriously doubted that Goldwater would enforce the Civil Rights Act; therefore, not so much in partisanship as in self-protection, many of the civil rights organizations discreetly opposed him. Now, however, CORE believes open political action, partisan and direct, is dictated.

There are several reasons for this new policy. Partly it is the outgrowth of an insight which has dawned on us in the midst of struggling these past years and which I discussed earlier in this book: the civil rights movement, we

now know, is not simply a means to achieve the status of
abstract equality; it is also a form of self-expression and self-
determination for America's Negroes and their brothers in
spirit. Negroes are passionately and self-interestedly de-
voted to civil rights for themselves—and, of course, for all
men. Without knowing it, the civil rights movement has
always been a political movement of Negroes, and when we
at CORE realized this, we decided that if we were to be
political we might as well do it in the most effective way
—by entering politics.

Until now, we have tended to make our political demands from outside of what we call the power structure.
"Do something for us, oh mighty power structure!"—
this in sum is what we said. And undeniably a lot of things
happened that way, including the expanding opportunity
to enter the political system as participants rather than be-
seechers.

Many of our objectives—job training and retraining,
elimination of slums, city planning for desegregation in
housing and schools, the elimination of political, educational, and cultural inequities—clearly will depend ultimately upon the political machinery, local, state, and federal. Men in motion, we have learned, generate power, but
there comes a time when pure motion must consolidate into
something more tangible and permanent. This consolida-
tion will produce self-conscious, purposive, well-organized
political structures. We must back up our cajolery with inside muscle.

This means much more than endorsing candidates on a
national level, though we must do that too, and endorse
and propose specific programs as well. More crucially, it
means endorsing candidates, *and running our own people*
on the local and state level (as an example, we can point
to the election of Archibald Hill, chairman of our Okla-

homa City CORE chapter, to the state legislature). It also means placing the right people in decision-making and planning positions in local, state, and federal agencies, and "infiltrating" party politics on a ward and precinct level.

I have spoken of "community organization" and CORE's determination to enter the Negro community—the ghettos of the North, the segregated towns of the South—and organize block by block, house by house. Inevitably, these community organizations must take a political form, for political action always results when people develop a collective sense of themselves and a collective will to achieve a better life. It is essential that these community organizations be truly local, with local leadership and a program which emanates from local needs. The field worker who sets out to organize a local group must learn not to superimpose his own idea of what the people ought to want upon their own idea of what they actually want. One cannot predict what set of priorities a community will establish. Better pavement, perhaps, or improved sewage disposal; a new playground, a safer street; a new traffic light; an alteration in school curriculum; more Negro policemen; honest housing inspectors; stricter supervision of cutthroat landlords; better-designed public housing; public works; a lessening of police brutality and a civilian review board (this is a blood-and-guts issue in every Negro settlement I know of). What is important is that whatever the program, it will be the expression of the people themselves, wishing, in the classic democratic tradition, a strong voice in governing themselves.

I emphasize local politics here because I believe that we are entering an era when local politics will be increasingly important. The government poverty program is committed to working within existing community institutions and organizations, and CORE must work to keep money which could be well spent from ending up in the pork barrel of some petty politico. Everywhere we will be registering voters, and with the swift enfranchisement of Negroes we can expect politicians to zero in on new voters. CORE will be an inside force resisting the inevitable graft and corruption, dismantling and paralyzing the oppressive political machines which will begin to emerge, helping develop sound leaders, challenging local tyrants.*

Students of the modern city are now saying that city governments are outmoded instruments for dealing with local problems. Metropolitan New York, for example, functions as one huge economic unit, yet it is governed by three states, hundreds of towns, and other overlapping authorities. Rationally, there should be no New York City, and in two or three decades we may witness, as Peter Drucker has predicted, a veritable revolution in local government. At the same time, if present trends continue, we shall see Negroes comprising the majority or near majority of several Northern cities: Philadelphia, New York, Detroit, Chicago, Newark, Los Angeles, Cleveland. Will the politicians seek to take power away from the center city just as Negroes come into prominence? It could happen. The fact is that there will be no major urban problem which will not touch the lives of Negroes and command their political attention. Clearly, we must be party to all local change.

CORE intends to mount political action in the South as well as the North, and indeed the best present examples of

---

* Republican John Lindsay would not have been elected Mayor of New York City without the 43 per cent of the Negro vote which largely switched from the Democratic column to support him. This kind of politically sophisticated vote switching also occurred in Philadelphia and Louisville, electing a District Attorney and Mayor, respectively. In Cleveland, Negro Assemblyman Carl Stokes received over eighty-five thousand votes and just barely missed being elected Mayor. The Negro vote is clearly no longer in any one political party's "bag."

the validity and effectiveness of this concept of political participation come from the South. In November, 1963, COFO, the covering civil rights organization in Mississippi, staffed predominantly with SNCC and CORE people, helped stage a mock election for governor in Mississippi to dramatize the desire of Mississippi Negroes to vote. Eighty thousand men and women voted in that election, risking the reprisal that any expression of political hope by a black man invites in Mississippi (about 7 per cent of the Negroes of voting age, twenty-three thousand people, were "legally" registered at that time). More than a dramatic gimmick to attract national attention, the mock election proved a superb educational device for instructing Mississippi Negroes in the ways and means of voting.

From this mock election sprang another idea, a little closer now to actual political participation. COFO helped organize a convention to found a Mississippi Freedom Democratic Party (FDP) which met on April 24, 1964. Since even those few Negroes who could register were excluded from the regular state Democratic Party, FDP decided to build a truly democratic Democratic Party, open to all Mississippians, white and black, with its delegates going then to the National Convention in Atlantic City in August, demanding accreditation as the state's legitimate Democratic Party. As proof of their popular support, they had the evidence of eighty thousand freedom votes; as indication of their loyalty to the party, they offered their pledge to the national ticket and the reminder that the regular party had abandoned Kennedy and Johnson in 1960. By early August, FDP was entrenched in forty counties, organized at local, county, and district levels, a replica of the organization of the regular party. Throughout the summer, helped by workers in the Summer Project, Mississippians began a massive freedom registration and local leaders began to take the helm of what was gradually becoming a full-fledged political party. At an FDP convention in early August, representatives from all over the state selected a delegation to represent them in Atlantic City and carefully instructed their representatives which compromises they should accept and which they should reject from the Democratic National Committee.

Interest was growing throughout the country, and several other state delegations announced their intention to support the seating of the FDP delegation. Liberal organizations, church and labor groups threw themselves into the fight. In a stirring presentation to the Credentials Committee, several FDP delegates told of their efforts to register, painting a picture of violent repression and inhumanity which seared the conscience of the Convention. The legal basis of their demands was admittedly a bit shaky, but its moral soundness was undeniable.

What happened then is well known. Eager to avoid a floor fight, the Convention offered a compromise: two designated FDP representatives would be seated as delegates-at-large; all members of the lily-white regulars who would sign a pledge to support the national ticket would be seated. Such respected figures as Martin Luther King, Bayard Rustin, and Joseph Rauh, the FDP counsel, advised the Mississippians to accept, and some of the Party's liberal supporters felt personally betrayed when FDP rejected their sage advice. The compromise was rejected by both FDP and the regular delegation. Was the FDP decision wise? There can be an honest difference of opinion on the question. But on one point there can be no difference: the decision was completely theirs to make. For myself, I felt that at that point in the emergence of the political sense in Mississippi, it was especially important that they make their own choice, and for that reason I kept my counsel.

In the fall of 1964 FDP ran three candidates for Congress and one for the Senate. Their candidates denied a place on the official ballot, FDP staged their own election, inviting all Mississippians who were registered, officially or unofficially, to vote. All candidates, including Mr. Goldwater, were listed on the ballot. Again nearly eighty thousand votes were tallied, and all the FDP candidates were elected. Goldwater got a few hundred votes, but then he didn't get many votes anywhere among Negroes.

After their election the three newly elected congressmen —actually, congresswomen: Fannie Lou Hamer, Annie Devine, and Victoria Gray—challenged the seating in the House of Representatives of the congressmen who had been elected in the "regular election" (definition of a "regular election" in Mississippi: an election from which 43 per cent of the population is excluded). In support of the challenge, FDP lawyers collected depositions from all over Mississippi, documenting indisputably the vicious denial of voting rights in Mississippi. And despite these efforts Congress chose to dismiss the "challenge" in 1965.

All this time, the FDP was meeting locally, discussing what was happening, designing plans for the future, preparing itself for the day soon to come when Negroes would enter the political life of Mississippi. For example, in some of the rural areas FDP organized sharecroppers to demand higher wages and better working conditions. The party is home-grown and home-led. It is a splendid example of the regeneration political participation can work in people.

The idea of a Freedom Democratic Party particularly suited Mississippi. I am not sure that it would be useful in other states. One obvious difficulty in FDP is that it ties all political effort to the Democratic Party. In most places Negroes will need a freer hand. But political organization of some sort is valid and CORE is now founding Freedom

Democratic Movements all over the North.* Not parties, these local movements will serve as flexible independent pressure groups, working where and when necessary against local political structures.

In Louisiana, CORE staff works in thirty parishes to develop local organization, local leadership. Three issues in particular are being emphasized: voting rights; civic conditions, including street repairs and mail delivery in Negro sections; and public accommodations. In South Carolina we are working intensively in voter registration, and in 1965 we have registered over twenty-seven thousand Negroes in the state. By the time of the 1966 elections, we expect to be able to run and elect several Negroes to local and state offices.

No one knows better than President Johnson the potential power of Negro votes in the South and across the nation. Negro voters swung the election to Johnson in Tennessee, Virginia, Florida, North Carolina, and Arkansas, and came close to swinging it in South Carolina, Georgia and Arizona. The President knows that if more Negroes were registered in these states he would have won them and that any gains he makes in Alabama and Mississippi will depend on massive Negro registration. Senator John Sparkman, Democrat of Alabama, will be running for re-election in 1966, and it will be interesting to see how vigorously Johnson prods the Justice Department to register voters who could re-elect his former colleague in the Senate. In about 150 counties in the South, Negroes comprise 50 per cent or more of the population, and in these places prompt registration of Negro voters could effect a revolution in the structure of local power. And, of course, in many

* For example, Major Owens, chairman of Brooklyn CORE, was a candidate for the City Council in the Democratic primary in September, 1965, running for the Brooklyn Freedom Democratic Movement.

Southern cities Negroes provide a crucial balance of power. The opportunities opened by the power of the vote are enormous and CORE will be very busy in the next few years, helping people to help themselves prepare for election day.

There is another type of election in the South which is no less significant in the lives of many Negroes. These are the elections held by the Department of Agriculture in which farmers, *including sharecroppers*, elect representatives who help determine and administer acreage allotments, subsidy payments, and other matters farmers think most about. As in all Southern matters the Negro has been largely excluded from these elections, though it must be conceded that many now do not participate out of ignorance and apathy. One of the tasks that CORE has been performing in Louisiana and Mississippi has been maintaining workers to apprize Negro farmers of their rights and opportunities. This is no simple matter. A minor revolution must occur in the heart of a sharecropper before he will risk voting in a county agricultural election.

Those Americans who are born to political privilege often have difficulty understanding how very hard it is to make a man into a political person—well enough informed, bold enough, hopeful enough to vote. By testifying about the difficulties they encountered and their success in overcoming these difficulties, the civil rights workers in the South could re-instruct this blasé country about how precious its heritage of political freedom really is. And one cannot overstress the point that the vote itself is meaningless unless it is used by trained citizens. The great value of the FDP and CORE community projects in the South is that they provide a kind of gymnasium where Negroes can limber up for citizenship. They provide an object lesson in CORE's basic principles: one becomes a free citizen by be-

ing a citizen; people must act for themselves; deputy leaders, "outside agitators," will fail if they do not develop
local leaders to carry on the work.

My greatest fear is that the motion we have set loose in
the South will be halted and that the Negro there will
drift again to the back of the bus. Writers are fond of saying (indeed rereading my chapter on Plaquemine I find myself saying), "whatever else happened—in the towns along
the route of the Freedom Rides, in Albany, Georgia, in
Meridian, Mississippi, and Plaquemine, Louisiana—this town
will never be the same again. Something has changed."
There was change in those towns, but it is not true that
they could never be the same again. They could be, if possibilities close and movement stops. We must maintain momentum, and we have learned that the one way to maintain and preserve momentum over a long period of time is
by building solid habits and institutions of political participation.

I have emphasized local politics. But I do not wish to
imply that beyond street lights and mail delivery and civilian review boards and mayoralty elections there are not
issues of national dimension touching local lives. One of
the tasks of National CORE will be to provide local chapters with materials which can help Negroes relate local
politics to national politics and beyond that (as I have
hinted in my discussion of Africa) to international politics.
Is the new voting law adequate, and is the Attorney General
enforcing it adequately? Should there be an expanded program of public works? Demonstrations by local unemployed
workers can make the point vividly. Has a President betrayed his trust? He'll hear from us in the election. Are
American banks underwriting apartheid in South Africa?
Local bodies will be present to picket them.

But it is important, too, to remember that National

CORE cannot force down local throats a program dictated by larger considerations. Political participation implies political independence. Negroes will demand what
they will demand and understand what is understandable
in the context of their lives. In offering these reflections, I
am thinking of a kind of tactician who lives around the
movement, constantly offering bold and far-reaching advice. We must have massive public planning and spending,
he will say. Poverty is the real problem. We must guarantee every man, employed or unemployed, a living wage.
Unemployment is no disgrace; we must develop values appropriate to an automated world. There must be a great
coalition of conscience uniting all the progressive forces of
society. Short of saying that poverty is a good thing, I can
think of no way to disagree with these sentiments, and
where feasible I believe they should be translated into action. But how, exactly, they translate into local programs
is difficult to say, and some of their advocates (and I'm
thinking now particularly of Bayard Rustin) have not said.
I believe the movement is doomed if it must immediately
begin discussing the impact of cybernetics every Thursday
at 8 P.M.

If one calls for local political participation, as Rustin
does, then he is inviting some chaos and obstinacy. There
will be repetitions of Atlantic City, where the people will
refuse to see what we geniuses are driving at. What will
CORE do when local groups develop programs which run
across the grain of these advanced philosophies? For example, many local CORE groups are attempting to help Negroes start small businesses. As I have said, the experts tell
us that the day of the small business is through in America
and suggest our people can better spend their time. How?
I ask. They do this well, and *they* do it. Again, some philosophers say that the Negro must forge an alliance with

the labor movement—because Negroes comprise only one tenth of the population. But does this mean that a local group—like our chapter in Detroit which picketed a striking printers' union for discriminating against Negroes—should honor all picket lines? As I have said, I agree fully that we must maintain an alliance with labor and church and liberal organizations. Indeed, we are powerfully allied with them now, and the alliance is strong enough to survive some tensions.

No decision in CORE's history has been more crucial or more dangerous than our decision to enter politics. Many petty politicians and grand ones will try to take over our local and regional organizations. Opportunistic individuals will join CORE to use it to further their own political ambitions. CORE members may fight CORE members in the sharp partisanship of political involvement and candidacies. Political parties will seek to make the organization an extension of themselves and adjuncts of their machinery. Yet I am convinced that we must run these risks.

III. COMMUNITY DEVELOPMENT

Political action, as we use the term, is a method of self-help. The kind of community organization and mobilization politics require will also provide the framework for CORE programs in remedial education, economic development, cultural enrichment.

Take remedial education. Many educators have commented about the low level of reading and mathematical skills among young Negroes sequestered in the ghetto. From these skills all educational things follow; without them the child falls helplessly behind. If expertise and professional technique alone could mend broken hearts and hopes, we might look to the educational establishment to upgrade the capacities of these youngsters. But it is clear to us that they suffer from that total conspiracy which has ripped so much of the fabric of American Negro life, and since the ghetto will be with us for a while, that they will not be mended until the ghetto is mended. Even if there were teachers available for them, the problem would remain that they distrust teachers and institutions.

In the next year there will be initiated a pilot program in remedial reading, using whatever buildings are available and non-teachers who are known in the community to instruct. We are now engaged in training ghetto personnel to master the Accelerated Progressive Choice Reading Program, developed by Myron Woolman of the Institute of Educational Research in Washington. The method developed by Dr. Woolman was designed specifically for use by relatively untrained personnel. It incorporates the learning-by-teaching approach. The content of the reading material can be tailored to meet the special vocabulary and requirements of the particular neighborhood, and it allows the student to advance as rapidly as his capabilities permit. I have seen this method in operation and was amazed at the interest, involvement, discipline, and motivation of both instructors and students.

The initial cadre of instructors will come from the active membership of community organizations. They will recruit their own students. Later, other community volunteers will be utilized; eventually we will use older students to instruct others. I observed student helpers giving instruction in a junior high school in North Carolina. The eighth-graders were almost as effective as the teachers, and if eighth-graders can teach reading to others, it becomes obvious that with proper supervision the number of potential teachers is enormous. Many bright ghetto youngsters have shown an eagerness to help.

We are extremely excited about prospects for this program throughout the country. But one point needs emphasis. The remedial-reading program can be effective only in the context of other community programs. It recommends itself not only as an effective technique but as one form of community expression in the context of a community learning to express itself. Our task will be to begin building that larger context. A remedial-reading program will have limited effect if there is no literacy course to permit the parent to keep up with his child. Both programs will have limited effect if the parents have no marketable skills and live in squalor. Relentlessly we will seek out local people to staff or at least assist in the projects the community chooses to mount.

What kind of programs can be developed within communities? Here is a list of some of the programs pursued by CORE community action projects throughout the country.

1. Remedial education, with particular emphasis on reading, writing, and arithmetic, comprehension and oral expression.
2. Academic counseling and vocational guidance.
3. Provision of after-school study centers, after-school tutoring, summer, weekend, and after-school classes.
4. Establishment of programs for preschool children.
5. Special services for disoriented migrant and transient families.
6. Provision of medical examinations and health education.
7. Rehabilitation and retraining of physically or mentally handicapped persons.
8. Provision of health, rehabilitation, employment, educational and related services to young men not qualified for military service.

9. Community child-care centers and youth activity centers.

10. Improvement of housing and living facilities and home-management skills.

11. Provision of recreation and physical-fitness services and facilities.

The impetus which will mount these programs, I repeat, must be part and parcel of the same impetus which will lead Negroes to vote or to protest and picket. I make no idle connection. The social-service mentality, enamored of its own techniques, filled with a lust to serve, invariably fails in the ghetto. We need people helping themselves, made healthy by the knowledge that the world is theirs, invigorated by their effort to make it just.

I stress the inalienability of political action from the total picture, because local communities will certainly be under heavy pressure to drop their political activities. Much of the money for community development will come from the government and foundations, and as much as the anti-poverty program and other programs may be committed to the ideal of community self-help, no government will be able to subsidize for too long what a congressman will call subversive. Most assuredly, the phone call will come into a CORE office: "Be practical, you know I'm on your side, you know how hard I've fought to preserve your independence. Call off the garbage-dump." "I can't," the answer must be, "it's not my decision, its theirs." It's a desperate dilemma. We need outside money, but not outside advice. And to complicate matters further, there will be Negroes and Negro organizations which will court favor with municipal and state and federal officials, angling for power, angling for approval. There is no simple solution, though there are some useful platitudes. We must be cautious and not be compromised by accepting support with strings attached. We must try to remain as self-sufficient as possible. We must not betray the people, not only because betrayal is dishonorable but because it undermines the freedom we are trying to build. There is no freedom without political self-expression.

And here I would speak of the cultural dimension of our efforts. I have spoken of the burgeoning sense of pride and self-identity among American Negroes—the identification with Africa, the sense of roots. Education is not simply a collection of skills; it must have a solid substance which resounds with meaning for the learner. When there is something to learn which, in the fullest sense, is about ourselves and for ourselves, we will learn. Until recently very little a ghetto child was asked to learn academically related in a valid way to his life. Not being free, he could make no history; unable to make history, he had no reason to learn it, or to learn anything. CORE intends to teach Negro history; and to study the world with an eye to the history our brothers are making; we will build libraries filled with *our* books, and we will write new ones. And recite *our* poetry, and write great new poems. We will produce plays, and exhibit our art, and dance as only we can dance. And we will make the American music, the Negro music, which is jazz, as Americans, as Negroes. We will be for ourselves, but not only for ourselves, for America, for mankind. And all of this is possible because we are making ourselves free.

IV

The title of this book asks the question, Freedom— When? In a way it is an outmoded question. A relic of those days when we dreamed of some apocalyptic end to our struggles. A flash of light perhaps, singing and weeping, the heavenly kingdom. But freedom is not an end: it is a beginning and a process. We feel further from the end now than we did before a decade's progress was wrought. We have settled down for a long haul. Things are not so clear as they once seemed, but the complexity is splendid; perhaps that is freedom too. We are overcoming. Maybe that is the sum of my reflections.

ABOUT THE AUTHOR

JAMES FARMER has been, since 1961, National Direc-
tor of CORE and before that Program Director of
NAACP. He was born on January 12, 1920, in Marshall,
Texas, and grew up there and in Mississippi and Georgia.
He studied theology at Howard University but refused
ordination, "I didn't see how I could honestly preach the
Gospel of Christ in a church that practiced discrimina-
tion." He was one of the founders of CORE in 1942.

Mr. Farmer now lives in New York City with his wife
and two young daughters.